ISBN 978-1-333-56490-2
PIBN 10520406

A BURMESE HISTORIAN OF BUDDHISM.

Dissertation

PRESENTED TO THE PHILOSOPHICAL FACULTY OF THE UNIVERSITY OF BERNE FOR THE DEGREE OF DOCTOR OF PHILOSOPHY

BY

MABEL HAYNES BODE.

PRINTED BY UNWIN BROTHERS,
WOKING AND LONDON

A BURMESE HISTORIAN OF BUDDHISM.

Dissertation

PRESENTED TO THE PHILOSOPHICAL FACULTY OF THE UNIVERSITY OF BERNE FOR THE DEGREE OF DOCTOR OF PHILOSOPHY

BY

MABEL HAYNES BODE.

Auf Antrag von Herrn Prof. Dr. E. Müller-Hess von der philosophischen Fakultät angenommen.

Bern, den 1 Juli 1898.

Der Dekan
Prof. Dr. Ed. Brückner.

PRINTED BY
UNWIN BROTHERS,
WOKING AND LONDON.

Dedicated

WITH THE AUTHOR'S LASTING GRATITUDE

TO

PROF. E. MÜLLER-HESS,

OF BERNE.

PREFACE.

THE following Dissertation is based on a Pali work edited by myself from MSS. in the British Museum. By the courtesy of M. Serge d'Oldenbourg (Professor of Sanskrit at St. Petersburg) I was able to collate my transcript with one made by the late Professor Minaev, who had obtained other MSS. from Ceylon. In the editing of the Text I have constantly referred my difficulties to Professor Müller-Hess, of Berne, who has added to countless kindnesses towards me, while I studied Sanskrit with him, that of reading the whole of the proof-sheets of the SĀSANAVAṂSA.

I wish to acknowledge most gratefully my debt as a student to the professors under whom I have worked during the past five years. My thanks are due to Professor Rhys Davids, who first led me to Oriental studies, and taught me Pali, to MM. les professeurs Sylvain Lévi, Victor Henry, and Louis Finot, of Paris; to Professor C. Bendall, of London; to Herr Professor Müller-Hess, and Herr Professor Woker, of Berne. That my teachers have constantly encouraged me to go forward is my best reward for my crude work, and its best apology.

M. H. B.

BERNE *July* 1, 1898.

CONTENTS.

	PAGE
Introduction	9
The Monks and Kings of Mramma	19
Conclusion	60
List of Principal Authorities Consulted ...	67

INTRODUCTION.

Among the modern works on Buddhism written by Buddhists is a Pali Text of Burmese authorship, entitled Sāsanavaṃsa. The Sāsanavaṃsa (now edited for the first time) has been known for many years to scholars. Prof. Kern in his recent *Manual of Indian Buddhism* (*Grundriss der Indo-arischen Philologie und Alterthumskunde*, III. Band, 8 Heft., p. 9) speaks of it as "highly important for the ecclesiastical history of Ceylon." The late Prof. Minaev's *Recherches sur le Bouddhisme* contains critical remarks on this text and several extracts (Appendices A and B to *Recherches*, also pp. 189, 208, 231, 232, 273). References to it occur in Childers' *Pali Dictionary*, and Prof. Hardy has drawn on it for his article *Ein Beitrag zur Frage ob Dhammapāla*, &c. Z.D.M.G., 51 Band, 1897. Louis de Zoysa, in his *Report on the Inspection of Temple Libraries in Ceylon* (1873), mentions the Sāsanavaṃsa as "a very interesting historical work." The author, Paññasāmi, who dates his book 1223 of the Burmese Common Era (1861 A.D.), was the tutor of the then reigning King Meng-dun-Meng, and himself a pupil of the Saṃgharājā, or Head of the Order, at Mandalay.

The *Mātikā* [table of contents] and opening chapter of the Sāsanavaṃsa seem to promise a general history of Buddhism. Beginning from the birth of the Buddha, the author gives a brief summary of the orthodox Siṅhalese tradition, drawn from a few well-known Pali works—

the ATṬHAKATHĀ (of the Mahāvihāra in Ceylon [1]), the SAMANTAPĀSĀDIKĀ,[2] (commentary of Buddhaghosa on the VINAYAPIṬAKÂ, the MAHĀVAṂSA and the DĪPAVAṂSA (Chronicles, historical and religious, of Ceylon). Events are brought up to the time of the Third Council in the time of AÇOKA PIYADASI [3] and the sending forth of Missionaries from Pāṭaliputra to nine different countries by the thera, MAHĀ-MOGGALIPUTTA-TISSA. The later history of religion is then followed in the countries mentioned, a separate chapter being given to each.

The whole of these nine chapters fall, roughly speaking, into two Books or Parts, by which division the scope of the Sāsanavaṃsa, as a History of Buddhism, becomes clear.

Part I., as we may call it (departing slightly from the order of the *Mātikā*), is a group of chapters of unequal length, mostly very short, and consisting of a few legends, strung together with quotations from Buddhaghosa and the Dīpavaṃsa.

The accounts of Sīhaḷa and Suvaṇṇabhūmi, however, show far more care and completeness, or we should rather say, more knowledge of the subject than the others of this group. That of Sīhaḷa is drawn chiefly from the same sources as the opening chapter, with some additions from a work of Burmese origin, *Buddhaghosuppatti.*[4] For Suvaṇṇabhūmi the author gives as his sources the ATṬHAKATHĀ, the RĀJAVAṂSA (probably the Pegu Chronicle), and lastly

---

[1] *Introduction* to Oldenberg's edition of the *Vinayapiṭakam*, p. xli.; Kern, *Manual Ind. Buddh.*, p. 110, *et seq.*

[2] Written some time between 410–432 A.D. Kern, *Man. Ind. Buddh.* p. 125.

[3] Dated 238 year of Religion in Chap. I. of the Sāsanavaṃsa, but 235 in Chapter II. (The Third Council is now placed at about 241 B.C. *Man. Ind. Buddh.*, p. 109).

[4] Edited and translated by Jas. Gray. London, 1892.

the Inscriptions—dating from the fifteenth century—of the celebrated KALYĀṆI SĪMĀ, the remains of which still exist in a suburb of Pegu city.[1]

Part II. is the longer and more important. It takes up about three-fifths of the book, but consists solely of Chapter VI., which treats of the history of religion in Aparanta, that is, in Mramma[2] or Burma proper.

Before this chapter is examined a few characteristic traits of Part I. should be pointed out.

The *résumé* of the early history of Buddhism (including the three Councils and the Great Schism, followed by the rise of seventeen sects, in the second century of Religion) is, as I have said, drawn from well-known Siṅhalese sources, but a few chronological details are added from Burmese history—or rather, legend. At the time of the First Council the mahāthera KASSAPA is said to have established the new era.[3] Further a certain JAMBUDĪPADHAJA[4] is named as the king reigning at Tagaung, the ancient capital of Upper Burma, in the time of

---

[1] The Text and Translation of the Inscriptions, edited by Taw Sein Ko, appeared in the *Indian Antiquary*, vol. xxii. (1893). See the same author's *Archæological Tour through Rāmaññadesa* (*Ind. Ant.*, vol. xxi. p. 383), and *Remarks on the Kalyāṇi Inscriptions* (*Ind. Ant.*, vol. xxiii., April, 1894).

[2] MRAMMA (Maramma or Myanmâ) see Phayre, *Hist. Bur. passim*. The derivation of the name is not yet settled; see Taw Sein Ko, *Folk-lore in Burma, Ind. Ant.* vol. xxii. p. 160, Note; also *Ind. Ant.*, vol. xxii. p. 30.

[3] According to Burmese tradition the era which was suppressed by Kassapa had been established 148 years before by the maternal grandfather of Gotama (Bp. Bigandet, *Life or Legend of Gaudama*, p. 361).

[4] See Sir Arthur Phayre's *History of Burma*, pp. 9, 276; A. Bastian's *Geschichte der Indo-Chinesen*, p. 12.

AJĀTAÇATRU, the friend of the Buddha; DVATTAPOṄKA [1] is mentioned as the contemporary of KĀLĀÇOKA, the former being king of Burma in the year 100 of Religion. Finally, the date of the Third Council is said to have fallen in the 12th year of the reign of RAṂPOṄKA,[2] King of Sirikhetta (Prome). The Section of Chapter I. that deals with the Missions may be said to strike the keynote of the Sāsanavaṃsa. The author gives a few explanatory notes on the Nine Regions visited by the first Missionaries, and, of these nine, five are placed in Indo-China. His horizon seems to be limited, first, by an orthodox desire to claim most of the early teachers for the countries of the *South* (and hence to prove the purest possible sources for the Southern doctrines); and, secondly, by a certain feeling of national pride. According to this account, Mahā-Moggaliputta Tissa (as if with a special care for the religious future of Mramma) sent two separate missionaries to neighbouring regions in the valley of the Irawaddy—besides three others, who visited Laos and Pegu.

A few geographical notes explain the nine regions (leaving out Sīhaḷa) as follows:—

SUVAṆṆABHŪMI is (as in the Aṭṭhakathā) identified with Sudhammapura—that is Thātōn at the mouth of the Sittaung River.[3]

---

[1] Dwottabaung 101 (Year of Religion). See Phayre's list of Kings of the Prome dynasty, *Hist. Bur.*, p. 277. The legend of Dwottabaung or Duttabaung (B.C. 442) is given in Taw Sein Ko's article *Folk-lore in Burma, Ind. Ant.*, vol. xxx. pp. 159 *et seq.*

[2] See Phayre's list (*His. Bur.*, p. 277). Ranbaung, sixth of the dynasty established at Tharekhet-ta-ra, reigned fifty years (from 193 to 243 Era of Religion). In Crawfurd's *Journal of an Embassy to the Court of Ava*, Appendix viii., a Burmese chronological table dates Ramb'haong, King of Prome, B.C. 351.

[3] SUVAṆṆABHŪMI see E. Forchhammer's *Notes on the*

YONAKARAṬṬHA is the country of the Yavana people or Jañ-May [1] (the country of the Shân tribes about Zimmé).

The identification of Paññasâmi is one to be met with commonly in the works of Burmese writers, according to whom *Yona* is the Shân country about Obieng-Mai (Taw Sein Ko, *Remarks*, &c.; Forchhammer, *Early History*, &c.). European authorities have unanimously placed Yonaka in the N. W. region of India invaded and held by the Greeks (see, among others, Rhys Davids, *Buddhism*, p. 227; Sylvain Lévi, *La Grèce et l'Inde*, p. 37; Max Duncker, *Geschichte der Arier*, p. 373).

In the chapter on Yonakaraṭṭha the author of the Sâsanavaṃsa localises the Yonaka country more exactly, mentioning the countries *Haribhuñja*, *Kamboja*, *Khemavara*, and *Ayuddha*, also the cities of *Sokkataya* and *Kapunna*. From these hints we may gather that his Yonaka country extends along the valleys of the *Me-nam* and *Me-ping* rivers and includes the Shân States to the north of these. The names *Kamphaung* and *Zimmé* (on the Meping) *Thukkate* and *Yuthia* (on the Me-nam) can be easily recognised under their pseudo-Pali forms.

Early *History and Geography of British Burma. The first Buddhist Mission to Suvaṇṇabhūmi* ; Taw Sein Ko, *Preliminary Study of the Kalyāṇi Inscriptions* (*Ind. Ant.* vol. xxii. p. 17) explains Sudhammanagara as the modern Thatôn in the Amhurst district. Phayre (*Hist. Bur.* p. 19) describes *Suvârnabhûmi* as including the delta of the Irawadi and *Thahtun* (being the capital) see also *op. cit.* p. 24, for references to Lassen, Yule, and Bp. Bigandet on Suvaṇṇabhūmi.

The chapter on Suvaṇṇabhūmi touches briefly on Religion in *Muttima* (Martaban) as a part of *Rāmañña*. The history of this region is only carried on to the year 1478 A.D. (reign of the celebrated King DHAMMACETI.)

[1] YONAKARAṬṬHA (The *Jañ-May* of the Pali MSS. of this work, is usually transcribed *Zimmé* or *Chieng-Mai*).

With regard to the *Yavana* people, it may further be noted that in the sketch map of the ancient classical divisions of Indo-China, in Lucien Fournereau's *Le Siam Ancien* (*Annales du Musée Guimet*, Tome 27) *Yavanadeça* lies to the east of the Me-ping River. For the Yavana people in Indo-China see also Abel Bergaigne's L'*ancien Royaume de Campâ d'après les* *Inscriptions*, p. 61, and *Mémoires et documents de la Mission Pavie*, p. 3.

The ancient *Haripunya* is identified by M. Fournereau with Lamphun (*Siam Ancien*, p. 53). M. Pavie says, describing a Thai inscription at Lamphun, "Ce *Hari*-puñjapura fut dans le haut Laos la station la plus reculèe vers la frontière de la Chine, et sans donte nous avons là la capitale du *Yavanadeça* qui du temps de la colonisation brahmanique comprenait la contrée du haut Mekhong, probablement toute le partie longeant la frontière de la Chine entre Chieng Mai et le Ton-king" (*Mémoires et documents de la Mission Pavie* (ed. M. Pavie et P. Lefèvre Pontalis), p. 144.

In the *Po: U: Daung Inscription* near Prome (ed. Taw Sein Ko, *Ind. Ant.*, vol. xxii. p. 1, *et seq*) the following states of the then Burmese kingdom are mentioned among others—*Kamboja* (including Moné, Nyangwé, Thibo and Alomeik), *Ayuttaya* (including Dvārāvati (Bangkok) Yodayā (Ayuthia) and Kamanpaik).

Khemavara, is the region including Kaington and Kyaing Kaung. It lies between the Saliwen and Me-kong rivers. (See also F. Garnier, *Voyage d'exploration en Indo-Chine*, p. 366; and Yule, *Mission to the Court of Ava*, p. 352.)

VANAVĀSI[1] (on which Western opinion has been divided)

---

[1] VAṄAVĀSI. Some opinions on *Vanavāsi* may be cited:—Childers (*Pali Dict.* s.v.) explains Vanavāso: "Name of a country. According to Vijesiṃiha it means Thibet."

Rhys Davids says (*Buddhism*, p. 227), "Vanavāsi, that

is the region round Prome. In support of this explanation the author mentions that an ancient image of the Buddha was found near Prome some years ago, the inscription of which says that it was erected for the homage of the people of *Vanavāsi*.

Of KASMĪRA-GANDHĀRA it is only said that these two countries formed part of one kingdom [*i.e.*, that of Açoka [1]] at the time of the Missions.

MAHIṂSAKAMAṆḌALA is (in agreement with other writers) identified as the Andhaka — or Andhra — country.[2]

CĪNARAṬṬHA, in the *Mātikā* of the Sāsanavaṃsa, takes the place of the *Himavantapadesa* of the Ceylon books.

---

is the wilderness. It surely cannot mean Thibet. . . . perhaps it was on the borders of the great desert in Rajputana."

Fergusson and Burgess (quoted by Taw Sein Ko in *Ind. Ant.*, vol. xxiii. p. 103) place Vanavāsi in Kanara (see *Cave Temples of India*, p. 17) and Köppen (*Religion des Buddha*, vol. i. pp. 195, 196) conjectures it to be "im Sudösten des heutigen Goa."

[1] KASMĪRA-GANDHĀRA. The Gandhāra country lay on the right bank of the Indus, south of Cabul (Max Duncker, *Geschichte der Arier*, p. 273).

[2] MAHIṂSAKAMAṆḌALA: Cf. the following:—

"*Mahīsamaṇḍala* worunter man vermuthet Mahīsmat oder Mahīsvara au der mitteren Nerbudda zu verstehen ist" (Köppen, *Rel. des Buddh.*, vol. i. p. 195).

Mahīsa, "the most southerly settlement of the Aryans South of the Godavari, in the Nizam's dominions" (Rh. Davids, *Buddhism*, p. 227, quoting Lassen's *Indische Alterthumskunde*, i. 681).

Mahīsamaṇḍala; Maisur (Fergusson and Burgess, *Cave Temples of India*, p. 17).

(Burma has its own *Mahimsakamaṇḍala*, a district,

Himavantapadesa, mentioned in our text as forming one region with Cīnaraṭṭha, has been identified with the Central Himalayas (Rh. Davids, *Buddhism*, p. 227), and with Nepâl (Fergusson and Burgess, *Cave Temples*, p. 17). The *Sen*, or *Chinarattha*, of the Po̊ Ů Daung Inscription is the borderland to the N.E. of Burma (*i.e*, includes the districts of Bhamo and Kaungsin, the district bordering on the Chinese province Yunnan). But in Chapter X. of the Sāsanavaṃsa, "On Religion in Cīnaraṭṭha," we read that the ruler of Cīna at one time ruled over Kasmīra-Gandhāra, though at the time of Majjhima's mission the latter countries did not form part of his domain. Kasmīra-Gandhāra did as a matter of fact become part of the great kingdom of the Mauryas in the time of Açoka (Max Duncker, *Geschichte der Arier*, pp. 275, 374), but at a later period war was waged between China and a rival power over these North-West provinces (Sylvain Lévi, *Notes sur les Indo-Scythes*, p. 62).

MAHĀRAṬṬHA is Mahānagararaṭṭha, or Siam.

MAHĀRAṬṬHA is considered by a number of European scholars to be the region of the Upper Godavari, that is, the country of the Mahārāstras (see E. Müller, *Journal of the Pāli Text Society*, 1888; also Rh. Davids, *Buddhism*, p. 227; Köppen, *Rel. Buddh.*, pp. 195, 196; Fergusson and Burgess, *Cave Temples*, p. 17). Childers, however, explains *Mahāraṭṭha* as Siam.

The author of the Sāsanavaṃsa explains that *his* Mahāraṭṭha or *Mahānagararaṭṭha* borders on Siam. From this observation and one or two others occurring in the chapter on Mahāraṭṭha, it would seem that the

---

mentioned in the *Po̊ Ů Daung Inscription*, including Mōgôk and Kyâtpyin).

It should be mentioned here that the name of the missionary to Mahiṃsaka is *Mahārevata* in Sās. V. *Mahādeva* in Dīpa V., Mahā. V., Suttav., Saddh. Saṃy., and Sām. Pas.

country in question is Laos. An interesting if slight allusion is made to the Brahmanic cult prevailing there at the time of the Mission (*aggihutādimicchākammaṃ yebhuyyena akaṃsu*). Nāgasena is mentioned as preaching in this region. (For Nāgasena in Laotian legend see Francis Garnier, *Voyage d'exploration*, pp. 248, 251. This author learnt that, in Siamese tradition, Laos is a Holy Land.) (*Op. cit.*, p. 100.)

I should add that an inscription of the seventeenth century, quoted by Burmese diplomatists in negotiation with the British Government and translated for his Government by Colonel Burney (Resident at Ava, 1837), thus defines the region *Mahānagara*, "All within the great districts of Kyaṃ-youn and Maṃgeen" (Yule, *Mission to the Court of Ava*, p. 351).

Finally, Aparantaraṭṭha (placed by European scholars west of the Punjab), is none other than the Sunāparanta of the Burmese, *i.e.*, the region lying west of the Upper Irawaddy.

It is best here to quote *verbatim* a passage from the Burmese scholar to whose researches I am indebted for so many facts: "The native writers of Burma, however, both lay and clerical, aver with great seriousness that the *Aparântaka* referred to is Burma Proper, which comprises the upper valley of the Irawaddy. . . . Such flagrantly erroneous identification of classical names has arisen from the national arrogance of the Burmans, who, after their conquest of the Talaing kingdoms on the seaboard, proceeded to invent new stories and classical names, so that they might not be outdone by the Talaings, who, according to their own history and traditions, received the Buddhist religion direct from missionaries from India. The right bank of the Irawaddy river near Pagan was accordingly renamed Sunāparanta, and identified with Aparântaka" (Taw Sein Ko, *Some Remarks on the Kalyāṇi Inscriptions*, *Ind. Ant.*, vol. xxiii. p. 103).

In the *British Burma Gazetteer* (vol. ii. p. 746)

Thoonaparanta is identified with the upper portion of the *Thayet* district, or the west bank of the Irawaddy.

"West" is the sense in which "Aparanta" has been taken as indicating a borderland west of the Punjab by European scholars, of whom I need only quote Professor Ed. Müller (*Journal of the Pali Text Society*, 1888), Professor Rhys Davids (*Buddhism*, p. 227), Kōppen (*Religion des Buddha*, vol. i. p. 192).

Tarānātha (p. 262 of Schiefner's translation) mentions Aparantaka as a part of India including "Bhangala and Odiviça."

The rest of Part I. of the Sāsanavaṃsa must be dismissed here with a few words. The religious history of the three regions outside Indo-China and Ceylon is not carried beyond the point where Buddhaghosa leaves it. To the brief account of the Aṭṭhakathā and the Dīpavaṃsa the Burmese author adds a few words of melancholy comment on the darkened state of those lands whence the sunlight of Religion has vanished. Mahāraṭṭha, Yonakaraṭṭha, and Vanavāsi are treated somewhat more fully, but these six chapters together made up only a small part of the book. I may add here that the Pali of the Sāsanavaṃsa also shows the author's intimate acquaintance with the commentaries. The style is plainly founded on that of Buddhaghosa and his successors. Naturally, in so modern a text there are no points of strictly philological interest. The obscurities that occur here and there may, I believe, be set down to the difficulties a Burman author would meet with in rendering into Pali some phrases characteristic of the Burmese language. Again, some words used by Paññasāmi in Part II. would appear to have a special application to the circumstances of his own country. It is this Part II., the most original and interesting chapter (on Religion in Aparanta), that is properly the subject of the present short study.

THE MONKS AND THE KINGS OF MRAMMA.

[In the following chapter the names and dates of the Kings of Burma *appearing in the text follow Paññasāmi; those in the notes are drawn from other sources (see authors cited) for comparison. Occasional references are given (by page) to the printed text of the Sāsanavaṃsa (published by the Pali Text Society).]*

In the Burma of to-day, as in the Europe of the Middle Ages, the monks are the historians; the last recension of the National Chronicle, or History of the Kings (Mahārājavaṃsa), was the work of "a body of learned monks and ex-monks" in the year 1824.[1]

But, though a lay point of view is hardly to be expected from such a body of editors, the native chronicles consulted by students of Burmese history have been described as very full and by no means untrustworthy.[2]

The Sāsanavaṃsa, a work of narrower scope, cannot, of course, add to our knowledge of the political and military

---

[1] See Taw Sein Ko's remarks on the native histories of Burma (*Indian Antiquary*), vol. xxii. p. 61.

Lassen (*Indische Alterthumskunde*), vol. iv. p. 369), writing in 1861, mentions a recension of the *Mahārājavaṃsa*, made by command of the king, some sixty years before. The work was based on two older histories. Among the works of the celebrated thera Aggadhammālaṃkara (17th century), mentioned in our text, occurs an abridged version (*Saṃkhepa*) of the *Rājavaṃsa*, written at the request of the king.

[2] See preface to Sir Arthur Phayre's *History of Burma*, London, 1883.

history of the author's country. Yet, in so far as the religion of the Buddha has played a great part in Burma's social life, and has been the first awakener of her intellectual life and the supreme interest controlling it, a record of the Order which, for centuries, has been the living embodiment of that religion, cannot but be interesting.

The RĀJAVAṂSA is one of the authorities frequently referred to (besides inscriptions and "ancient books") by the author of the SĀSANAVAṂSA, but he chooses from his material with a very strict regard for the purpose of his book. The National Chronicle is quoted here and there, but, as a whole, the part history plays in the religious records is slight. We find here only abrupt mention of wars and sieges, and allusions to kings of Burma, who serve as chronological milestones by the way, or stand out as pillars of the Religion, if they spend liberally to do it honour.

Paññāsāmi's history is a purely ecclesiastical piece of work. Kings are judged, as a rule, according to their "acts of merit"—the building of cetiyas and vihāras and the supporting of the Saṃgha—with a certain calm detachment, that is able to separate their names from any other associations, and to measure their virtue and importance by a measure of its own.

In the following analysis of the Sixth Chapter of the SĀSANAVAṂSA I have set set side by side with such hints of history—bare dates and scanty facts—as occur there, some references to the national chronicle.[1] Occasionally

---

[1] That is to such translations or abstracts as were accessible to me in the works of European writers, namely, Sir Arthur Phayre (*History of Burma*), Bishop Bigandet (*Life or Legend of Gaudama*), Sir H. Yule (*Narrative of a Mission to the Court of Ava*), J. Crawfurd (*Journal*), A. Bastian (*Geschichte der Indo-Chinesen*), Father San Germano (*The Burmese Empire*, ed. Jardine),

there is a curious and characteristic difference between the ecclesiastic's version and that of the kings' chroniclers. I have been compelled to leave out the picturesque element brought into the Mramma chapter by the stories told of noteworthy theras. The historical thread is broken by these side-episodes, and some of the chief points obscured, which a closer drawing together of the more important events may serve to bring out clearly.

The History of Religion in Mramma begins with a legendary visit of the Buddha himself[1] to the Lohitacandana vihāra (presented by the brothers Mahāpuṇṇa and Cūlapuṇṇa of Vānijagāma).[2] The Faith was not "established" in the land till the mission to Aparantaraṭṭha in the year 235 after the *Parinirvāna*,[3] but the historian mentions communities of bhikkhus as already existing in Aparanta when Yonakadhammarakkhita arrived and points out that the Sutta preached by that thera —the "Aggikkhandhopama"[4]—has a special bearing on the duties of bhikkhus. In this connection he refers, for the first time, to the heretics called Samaṇakuttakas,[5]

Taw Sein Ko (*Indian Antiquary*, vols. xxii. and xxiii.), E. Forchhammer (*Reports to the Government*), *British Burma Gazetteer*, Col. Burney's articles in *J. A. S. Bengal*, vol. iv., &c., &c.

[1] Cf. Spence Hardy, *Manual of Buddhism*, pp. 215 and 268.

[2] Lègaing (Taw Sein Ko, *Indian Antiquary*, vol. xxii. p. 6).

[3] The Burmese tradition places the Parinirvāna at 543–544 B.C.

[4] A discourse in the Suttanipāta (not yet edited) of the Aṅguttara Nikāya. I owe this reference to Prof. E. Hardy, editor of the Aṅguttara (together with other kind help in my study of the Sāsanavaṃsa).

[5] It is certain that the Buddhism of Burma fell away from purity at an early time. Positive evidence exists of

who are said to have gained a footing in Arimaddana (Pugân) even at that early period.

To give Arimaddana due religious importance from the earliest times, another legend is quoted here from the Ancient Books (*porāṇapotthakā*), telling how the Buddha visited a spot in Tambadīpa [1] and prophesied that SAMMUTIRĀJĀ [2] would build a city there, and religion would stand fast in that city.

To prove that Yonakadhammarakkita preached in Tambadīpa as well as in Aparanta, Paññasāmi points out that it is said in the Aṭṭhakathā that thousands of persons of the Kṣatriya clan were converted and entered the

---

the great changes that had come over the religion of the people by the eleventh century, at which time "a debased form of Buddhism which was probably introduced from Northern India existed at Pagân. Its teachers, called Aris, were not strict observers of their vow of celibacy, and it is expressly recorded in native histories that they had written records of their doctrines, the basis of which was that sin could be expiated by the recital of certain hymns" (Taw Sein Ko, *Ind. Ant.*, vol. xxiii. p. 258). The writer I quote refers, in another place, to ancient inscriptions in Burma as pointing to the influence of the Northern School of Buddhism (*Ind. Ant.*, vol. xxii. p. 165).

[1] According to the inscription translated by Col. Burney (see above), Tambadīpa includes the districts of Pugân, Ava, Panyâ, and Myenzain. In the *British Burma Gazetteer* (vol. ii., p. 746) Tambadīpa is described as the upper portion of the Thayet district, on the east bank of the Irawaddy.

[2] This King (SAMUDRI, THAMUGDARIT, THAMUDIRIT or THAMOONDIRIT) established a dynasty at Pugân in 108 A.D. (Phayre, *History of Burma*, p. 278. *Brit. Bur. Gazetteer*, Article "*History*," vol. i. p. 239; Burney Notice of Pugân, *J. A. S., Bengal*, vol. iv. p. 400).

Order, and, since there were no Kṣatriyas in Aparanta, this statement points to a visit of Yonakadhammarakkita to the neighbouring province, Tambadīpa.[1]

But though Arimaddana was destined to be a centre of religion, heresy was rife there from the time of Sammuti himself, and continued to grow and multiply till in the time of ANURUDDHA[2] the adherents of the Samaṇakuttakas numbered many thousands. The chief and most dangerous heresy of this sect is briefly described; it lies in the boundless abuse of the *Paritta*,[3] which becomes, with these heretics, a charm to absolve from guilt even the murderer of mother or father. Such doctrines (together with others that raised the ācariyas to tyrannical power over the family life of the laity[4]) had corrupted the

---

[1] Taw Sein Ko observes: "The finding among the ruins of Tagaung of terracotta tablets bearing Sanskrit legends affords some corroboration of the statement of the native historians that long before Anorat'azo's conquest of Thatôn, in the eleventh century A.D. successive waves of emigration from Gangetic India had passed through Manipur to the upper valley of the Irrawady, and that these emigrants brought with them letters, religion, and other elements of civilisation" (*Ind. Ant.*, voll. xxv. p. 7). For the same opinion see Phayre, *Hist. Bur.* (pp. 15, 16), and Forchhammer's *Notes on the Early History and Geography of British Burma*, p. 6.

[2] Anoarahtā, consecrated King in 1010 A.D. He is the great hero of the Burmese. (Phayre, *Hist. Bur.*, p. 22); A. Bastian, *Geschichte der Indo-Chinesen*, p. 33).

[3] Originally hymns, suttas and auspicious texts to ward off danger and evil spirits. (Childers, *Pali Dictionary*, s.v.; C. Bendall, *Catalogue of Sanskrit and Pali Books*, in the British Museum, 1892.)

[4] Sir Arthur Phayre, writing of this period, says that a change, from some unknown external cause, had corrupted religion in Burma—a change such as had already taken place in the Buddhism of the Punjab in the sixth century.

religion of Tambadīpa, when in the eleventh century a

He, too, gives the name "Ari" as that by which the heretics were known. Might not this *Ari* be a slightly altered form of the Sanskrit *arya*, the *Arya* of Buddhist terminology?

A further comparison of the Samaṇakuttaka heresy (very briefly summed up in the Sāsanavaṃsa) with the North Indian or rather Tibetan Buddhism, is suggested to me by the following sentences in our text: "Sace pi puttadhītānaṃ āvāhavivāhakammaṁ kattukāmo bhaveyya ācariyānaṃ paṭhamaṃ niyyādetvā āvāhavivāhakammaṃ kattabbaṃ; yo idam cārittam atikkameyya bahu apuññaṁ pasaveyyā ti." ("If any man be desirous of giving sons or daughters in marriage, he must first hand over (one of his offspring) to the ācariyas before (any) giving in marriage. Whosoever transgresses this rule commits great sin (lit. produces great demerit).") If my interpretation is correct (making niyyādetva refer to a direct object, understood from the puttadhītānam preceding) the passage recalls a trait of Tibetan Buddhism. "It would appear that compulsion is also exercised by the despotic priestly government in the shape of a recognised tax of children, to be made *lāmas*, named *btsun-gral*. Every family thus affords at least one of its sons to the church. The first born or favourite son is usually so dedicated in Tibet. The other son marries in order to continue the family name and inheritance. . . ." (L. A. Waddell's *Buddhism of Tibet*, p. 70).

I ought to add, however, that there is no mention in the Sāsanavaṃsa of Nāga-worship, as a practice of the Samaṇakuttakas, but Phayre's authority describes the Aris (the priests of this corrupt cult), living in monasteries like Buddhist monks. They were expelled and stripped of their robes (like the Samaṇakuttakas) when Anuruddha had come under the influence of "Arahân" from Thahtun (*Hist. Bur.*, p. 33).

With regard to the name Samaṇakuttaka: from the

new era opened with the arrival of the great thera Arahanta, from Thatōn.[1]

Arahanta's coming to Arimaddana, and the sweeping reforms that King Anuruddha forthwith carried out at his instance, are related with a fulness that shows how momentous this episode is in the eyes of the historian. [The story is first told in the words of the RĀJAVAṂSA, but two other versions follow, drawn from the PARIT-

---

analogy with *Kuttima* = artificial (derived by Childers from Skt. *Kṛtṛma*), *kuttaka* seems to be the Skt. *Kṛtaka* = false, artificial, simulated. *Samaṇakuttaka* would therefore simply mean: simulating (the life of) the Samaṇas. It is expressly said that the outward show of a monastic life like the Buddhist monks was kept up by this sect, and that the kings who patronised them believed them to be disciples of Gotama. Professor E. Müller has kindly pointed out to me an instance of the use of this adjective in the passage, "kuttakan ti solasannaṃ nâṭakitthînaṃ ṭhatvâ naecanayoggan uṇṇâmayattharaṇaṃ" (*Sumaṅgalavilâsinî*, I. p. 87). Here an artificial carpet is meant, affording room to sixteen dancing girls.

Discussing the term *Çramaṇakṛtakaḥ*, Prof. Bendall writes: "There are plenty of mentions of 'false Samaṇas' . . ." For a modern use of a similar phrase, I may also refer to a passage in Mr. Bird's valuable work, *Wanderings in Burma*, where he speaks of the modern clergy in the Eastern Shân States as "less orthodox than those in the Western States and Burma," who call them "*Htu*" or "*Imitation priests*." (See p. 23 of *Wanderings in Burma*. George Bird, Education Department, Burma, London, 1897.)

[1] The capital of Pegu, mentioned, in the text, by its classical Pali name Sudhammapura (see Taw Sein Ko, *Preliminary Study of the Kalyāṇi Inscriptions*, *Ind. Ant.*, vol. xxii. p. 17; Phayre, *Hist. Bur.*, p. 34).

TANIDĀNA and SĀSANAPAVEṆI[1].] The Samaṇakuttakas' heresy was, in fact, annihilated and their communities were relentlessly broken up, but Arahanta warned the king that there was danger for the future of religion, since no relics of the Master's body were treasured in the capital, and the sacred Texts were wanting. He therefore urged Anuruddha to send an embassy to Sudhammapura where there was a wealth of relics and books. This was done, but MANOHARI,[2] king of Pegu (jealous, as it is said—perhaps envying Anuruddha the honour of Arahanta's intimacy), refused the request, with a contempt that roused the Burmese king to fury.[3] He descended on Sudhammapura with a huge land force and a number of ships, and laid siege to the city. For a while the army was miracu-

---

[1] I have not come across the titles of these two works in any catalogue of Pali books or MSS. that I have been able to consult. They may be Burmese works, mentioned here by a classical instead of their vernacular name (according to Paññasāmi's usual custom). I may note that the difference between the three versions is characteristic. The *Rājavaṃsa* naturally brings the king into the foreground; the *Parittanidāna* tells the story of the thera's successful attack on the chief heresy of the Samaṇakuttakas, his exposure of a false miracle, and the burning of a book of false doctrine, while the *Sāsanapaveṇi* lays stress on Arahanta's place in the succession of theras.

[2] See Preliminary *Study of the Kalyāṇi* Inscriptions, *Ind. Ant.*, vol. xxii. p. 17. Manohari is also called Manuba (Phayre, *Hist. Bur.*, p. 34).

[3] The words of the message are given—a home thrust at Anuruddha's former patronage of heretics: "It is not seemly to send the three piṭakas and relics to such as you, who hold false doctrine—even as the fat of the maned lion can be kept in a bowl of gold and not in a vessel of clay." A proverb turning on this folk-superstition occurs in

lously prevented from approaching, but when Anuruddha's Brahman soothsayers,[1] skilled in the Atharvaveda, came to the rescue, the protecting spell was broken by the finding of the mutilated body of a murdered Hindu, buried under the city walls.[2] It was dug up and thrown into the sea and the besiegers entered Sudhammapura.

Manohari and all his household were carried away captive, and with his captives Anuruddha brought back to Pugân many elephant-loads of relics and books. All the members of the Saṃgha in Thatôn were transferred to Pugân, so that there were now a thousand teachers to

---

the well-known *Dhammaniti* of Burma (Section V., v. 62).

> Sīhamedā suvaṇṇena na ca tiṭṭhanti rajate
> Paṇḍitānaṃ kathāvākyaṃ na ca tiṭṭhati dujjane.

The superstition is that the fat of the lion evaporates if placed in a common vessel. (See Jas. Gray's *Nīti Literature of Burma*, p. 51.)

[1] For the employment of Brahmanical astrologers at the court of Burmese kings see Taw Sein Ko, *The Spiritual World of the Burmese* (*Transactions of the* Ninth *International* Congress *of Orientalists*, p. 179).

[2] "The Burmese kings of old used to have human beings buried alive at the four corners of the walls of their capital city at the time of its foundation, in order that the spirits of the deceased might keep watch and ward over the population, and by their occult influence fail the attempts of invaders to force an entrance into the city" (Taw Sein Ko, *Spiritual World*, &c., *Trans. Int. Con. Or.*, vol. x. p. 180).

Cf. A. Hillebrandt: "Weit verbreitet ist das Glaube dass ein Bau nur wohl befestigt sei wenn ein Mensch oder Tier in seine Fundamente gegraben ist" (*Vedische Opfer und Zauber. Grundriss der Indo-arischen Philologie u. Alterthumskunde.* 1. Band, 2 Heft, p. 9).

expound the sacred texts. Anuruddha further sent for copies from Ceylon, which Arahanta compared with those of Pegu, to settle the readings. Manohari is said to have been made a pagoda-slave,[1] but there is some evidence in the Sāsanavaṃsa that he was not ungenerously treated,[2] for while at Arimaddana he still possessed at least one of his royal jewels, a splendid gem, the price of which he devoted to the making of two great statues of the Buddha. According to Paññasāmi the statues exist to this day.

The Sāsanavaṃsa here leaves Anuruddha [3] and passes on to the time of NARAPATISISU [4] (1167 A.D.) The celebrated teacher Uttarājīva had come from Sudhammapura to Arimaddana and, in his turn, had established religion there. His pupil Chapada spent ten years studying in Ceylon, and then returned with four colleagues—Sīvali, Tamalinda, Rāhula, and Ānanda—to

---

[1] Phayre, *Hist. Bur.*, p. 34.

[2] Forchhammer, describing the so-called "Palace of Manuha," in his report of the ruins of Pugân, observes: "Anuruddha seems to have allowed Manuba the semblance at least of a king" (*Report*, Jan., 1891, pp. 7 and 8). Bird, *Wanderings*, &c., p. 353.

[3] Anuruddha's later attempts to get relics (from China and Ceylon) seem to have been less successful than his raid on Sudhammapura. (Phayre, *Hist. Bur.*, p. 35; Bastian, *Gesch. Ind. Chin.*, pp. 33, 38.)

[4] Narabadi-tsi-tsi-thu (1167). Six kings, the earlier successors of Anuruddha, are here passed over. Two of them are mentioned in the text further on. (See Phayre, *Hist. Bur.*, pp. 37, 49, 281.)

"Vielleicht erst mit Narapadisethu wird wieder geschichtlicher Boden getreten" (Bastian, *Gesch. Ind. Chin.*, p. 35).

the capital.[1] There they set up a community apart,[2] and were specially favoured by King Narapati. After the death of Chapada separate schools came into existence, having their origin in certain differences[3] that arose between the three surviving teachers—Sīvah, Tamalinda, and Ānanda (p. 66), Rāhula having already quitted the Order.

The schools were named each after its leader, but are together known as the *pacchāgaṇa* (or later school) to distinguish them from the earlier school in Arimaddana *(purimagaṇa)* founded by Arahanta (p. 67).

The three teachers died early in the thirteenth century, a time when, it is said, religion shone at its brightest in Pugân. A short digression is made here to mention the building of the celebrated Nanda (or Ananda) temple by King CHATTAGUHINDA [4] (p. 68) in the eleventh century, and the history then returns to the time of NARAPATI,[5]

---

[1] The whole story is related in the Kalyāṇi Inscriptions. (See Taw Sein Ko, *Preliminary Study*, &c. *Ind. Ant.*, vol. xxii. p. 29, *et. seq.*)

[2] Narapati assigned separate quarters to the different sects then flourishing at Pugân. (See Forchhammer's Archæological Report, 1891.)

[3] They disagreed on the application of Vinaya rules to the following cases: The keeping of a tame elephant, received as a present from the king (instead of setting it at liberty), and the personal recommending of pupils by a teacher *(Vaciviññatti)*.

[4] *Kyansitthâ* (1057 A.D.). (Phayre, *Hist. Bur.*, pp. 39, 281.) For descriptions of the still-frequented Ananda temple see Yule, *Mission to the Court of Ava*, p. 36, and Crawfurd's *Journal*, p. 114.

[5] It is rather curious that only one passing mention occurs in the text, of ALON-CAÑ-ÑU (Alaungsithu, 1058 A.D.), the grandson of Kyansitthâ, a notable king and a zealous Buddhist. He built the great Shwe-ku temple at

(p. 69), a king whose personality stands out with some distinctness in a story of the thera Sīlabuddhi. We see in this latter one of the best types of the Buddhist monk unspoilt by kingly favour as untouched by spiritual pride He opposes the sovereign's wish to build a cetiya on the Khanitthipâda hill, warning him that there is no merit in forcing on his people the heavy labour of levelling the ground. He refuses to eat of the king's bread, and would leave for Sīhaḷa but is prevented, by a stratagem of a resourceful minister, and brought back to the king. Narapati, warned by the haunting of a terrifying *Yaksha*, that he has erred, receives the holy man with great honour, and hands over to him his five sons. Sīlabuddhi's characteristic response is to trace out five sites where his royal bondsmen shall build five cetiyas, and with that act he restores them their freedom.

Other anecdotes follow to illustrate the splendour of religion in Arimaddana and its continuance through Saints and Arhats.[1] The author adds that he could relate many more, but that he fears to overload his history (p. 72).

Pugân, improved the administration of law in his kingdom, interfered successfully in the affairs of Arakan, and caused the Buddhist temple at Gaya to be repaired, where an inscription testifies to his piety (see Phayre, *Hist. Bur.*, p. 39). Some explanation of this silence may, perhaps, be found in a fact noted by Bastian (*Gesch. Ind. Chin.*, p. 38), namely, that the personalities of Anoarahtâ and Alaungsithu have become mingled in Burmese tradition (to the profit of the greater hero's reputation).

[1] The difficulty of recognising the arhat in this world is briefly discussed here. Examples of abstract questions in the Sāsanavaṃsa are so rare that I mention this instance. An anecdote relating to arhatship is told of Mahākassapa, whose attainment to that state was not recognised by his *saddhivihārika*, the pupil who was his daily attendant.

On the anecdotes follows an account of the RELIGIOUS LITERATURE of Tambadīpa, the beginning of which is traced back to the reign of SAṄ-LAṄ-KROṄ rājā[1] contemporary of Mahānāma of Sīhaḷa. The mahātheras of Mramma were already writing books in the time of Buddhaghosa and Buddhadatta, and ṭīkas were composed by later authors, for the full understanding of the ancient works. In the year 1127, Aggavaṃsa wrote the celebrated grammatical treatise *Saddanīti*[2] expounding the original meaning of the language used in the three Piṭakas. Siṅhalese scholars of that time, we are told, said of this work that they had none in their own country to compare with it, in settling difficult points.

Other works of the twelfth and thirteenth centuries are mentioned, with the names of their authors. Prominence is given to books on grammar, and here the name of Saddhammakitti is marked out for special honour as the author of the EKAKKHARAKOSA.[3] Saddhammakitti lived in the troublous times when religion languished in Tambadīpa under the cruel rule of a heretic of the JALUMA family.[4] The Ekakkharakosa was written to keep alive B.E. 887.

The story of Pilinda vaccha is referred to (see *Suttavibhaṇga*, xxiii. 1, and Iddhikathā of Kathāvatthu, xxi. 4).

The digression leads up to the statement that the theras Sīhaḷabuddhi, Polloṅka, and Sumedha of Arimaddana were arhats.

[1] THENG-LAY-GYUNG, about 345 A.D. (*Rajaweng* list of Kings of Pugân. Phayre's *Hist. Bur.*, p. 279).

[2] Forchhammer's Archæological Report on Pugân, p. 2.

[3] *Ekakkharakosa*, a small vocabulary of words of various significations ending in certain final letters, compiled by a very learned Buddhist priest of Burma named Saddhammakitti. [Subhūti, preface to his edition of *Ekakkharakosa*, edited with *Abhidhānappadīpikā*, Colombo, 1883.]

[4] A son of the Shân chief and conqueror of Ava, SALUN or Tsalun. Ava was taken by the Shâns about 1523, and Salun placed his son THO-HAN-BWA on the throne. Under

sacred learning, then in mortal danger from the great destruction of books in the land (p. 76).

From Saddhammakitti's time, the beginning of the sixteenth century, the story again goes back to the later Kings of Pugân. Of King JEYYASIṄKHA (1219 A.D.),[1] we only hear that he forsakes the world, broken-hearted at
L. 581. the death of a son, and is succeeded by Kyocvā. The latter's piety and zealous furthering of religion are enthusiastically praised.[2] Plunged in study he left the affairs of state to his son: he was himself the author of two manuals, *Paramatthabindu* and *Saddabindu*, for the use of his wives, and one of his daughters wrote the *Vibhatyattha*.[3] It was even currently said that this king, in a former existence, had been the mighty champion of religion, Anuruddha.

---

him the Buddhist monks suffered a ruthless persecution (see Phayre, *Hist. Bur.*, p. 93, and *British Burma Gazetteer*, vol. i. p. 278).

[1] According to Phayre's authorities Jeyyasiṅkha succeeded his father in 1204, and his reign came to an end in 1227. His son Kyocvā or Kyatswâ appears in Phayre's list of Kings (*Hist. Bur.*, p. 281), but there is no further account of him. It was at this period that "danger began to gather round the Pugân monarchy" (Phayre, *Hist. Bur.*, p. 51).

[2] A Burman Chronicle, quoted by Crawfurd (Journal, vol. ii., p. 288), says of Kyocvā, "He loved everybody, read and became master of every book, held public disputations, and seven times a day instructed his household. He wrote himself a work called Parmata Bingdu, and built a great house for the purpose of holding disputations. He also constructed a monastery at Sagu and a great tank by damming a mountain stream. During this reign there were no wars or commotions of any kind. . . ."

[3] *Vibhatyattha* affords examples of the Pali cases. (Subhūti, preface to *Abhidhanappadīpikā*.)

The career of the thera Dīsapamokkha, who attained to profound knowledge in his old age, illustrates these golden days of learning under Kyocvā. The story is followed by a glowing account of the science and zeal of the women of Arimaddana, and anecdotes are told of their skill in grammar and the keenness of their wit [1] (p.78). On this joyous note the history of religion in Arimaddana ends. There is no mention of Kyocvā's next successors. UZANA (1243 A.D.) and NARATHIHAPATÉ (1248). (Phayre, *Hist. Bur.*, p. 281.) Bastian quotes an inscription in Sagain which mentions *Nara-siha-pade*, under whom the temples of Pugān were torn down to fortify the city against the Chinese (*Gesch. Ind. Chin.*, p. 41). Even the building of a gorgeous cetiya does not earn a place for NARATHIHAPATÉ among the kings of the Sāsanavaṃsa. The Burmese people remember him as TARUK-PYE-MENG, a nickname that keeps alive only the memory of his unkingly flight from his capital before the Taruk; and in the eyes of the monks the "merit" of the great cetiya may well have been lost to its founder, when the temples of Arimaddana were torn down in a vain attempt to fortify the city against the Mongol invaders.[2]

The centre of interest now shifts from Tambadīpa to Ketumatī, the capital of Jeyyavaḍḍhana [3] and the history suddenly passes over to a later period (1510 A.D.) (p. 80). The founding of Ketumatī by king MAHĀSIRIJEYYASŪRA,[4]

---

[1] An extract from this part of the Mramma chapter is given by Minaev in Appendix B to Chapter III. of his *Recherches sur le Bouddhisme.*

[2] Phayre, *Hist. Bur.*, pp. 51, 53, 54; and Col. Burney's translations from *Rājavaṃsa*. J. A. S. Bengal, vol. iv. p. 400, *et seq*. Bird, *Wanderings*, p. 121.

[3] Taungu. (*Ind. Ant.*, vol. xxii. p. 4, &c.)

[4] MENG KYÎNYO, who assassinated his uncle and succeeded him in 1845. He founded Taungu city. Phayre, *Hist. Bur.*, p. 92, and Mason (abstract from the chronicles of Taungu) in *Burma*, p. 65.

a descendant of the fallen dynasty of Pugân, and the steady growth of his power, as a rival to the Shân usurpers then ruling in Tambadīpa, give a historical importance to his reign, but it is naturally not for this reason that it stands out in the annals of religion. The events chronicled in the Sāsanavaṃsa are the arrival, in the year 1530, of the thera Mahāparakkama from Ceylon, and the breaking out of a controversy which he was afterwards called upon to decide. The dispute was about the precept (*sikkhāpada*) relating to intoxicating drinks.[1] The disputing parties differed in their interpretation of passages in the *Kaṅkhāvitaraṇi*,[2] and other commentaries, dealing with the question: at what stage of its preparation the juice of the coconut palm, &c. [*tāli-nāli-kerādīnaṃ*], should be considered an intoxicating [and therefore unlawful] drink. Mahāparakkama gave judgment and afterwards wrote the book called *Surāvinicchaya* on this same question.

Here another change of period takes us back more than two hundred years to the last days of the hapless KITTITARA,[3] the deposed king of Pugân. The scene is again Tambadīpa, but Arimaddana is no longer the citadel of religion. A blank is left between the reign of the pious KYOCVĀ I. and that of the three Shân usurpers, who
664 now (1302 A.D.) hold the last king of Pugân prisoner at Khandhapura.[4] One episode alone brings Khandhapura into the History of Religion, namely, the siege of the city by a Mongol army, at the instance of the Burmese king's

---

[1] One of the five that are binding on every Buddhist. (Rhys Davids, *Buddhism*, pp. 139, 140.)

[2] Buddhaghosa's Commentary on the Pātimokkha.

[3] KYOSWÂ or KYAUTSWA II. (1279 A.D.). *Hist. Bur.*, pp. 58, 281.

[4] Myinzaing, a few miles to the south of Ava. (See *Hist. Bur.*, p. 58, and Col. Burney's Translation (*loc. sit.*) for the Rājavaṃsa account of this episode. It agrees in its main features with that given in Sāsanavaṃsa.)

son, who sought to restore his father to power. According to the Sāsanavaṃsa the Shān brothers, at the time of the siege, sought the advice of a learned thera, as to their best tactics, and received the rather sarcastic answer that such affairs were not the province of the Samaṇa and they had better consult the actors (p. 82). The brothers followed this counsel to the letter, took the song of some actors, in a water-spectacle, as a hint to be acted upon, and killed their captive. The besiegers then withdrew, holding it useless to carry on the war on behalf of a dead man.

According to Burmese chronicles a monastery was built at Khandhapura by the Shān governors,[1] but this is not mentioned in the Sāsanavaṃsa, where it is only stated that a number of theras dwelt in the city, but no books were written there.

The youngest of the three Shān brothers, however—SĪHASŪRA[2]—finds a place in our history as the founder of the capital Vijayapura[3] (in 1312) and as a protector of religion. Yet in his reign there were few righteous bhikkhus and the Samaṇakuttaka heresy revived. Better days followed in the reign of his adopted son UJANA[4] (1322) who built seven great cetiyas and bestowed gifts of land with them. Religion flourished then in Vijayapura, for many thousands of theras had settled there; nevertheless, a scandal was caused by the quarrels of the bhikkhus appointed to receive from the tillers of the soil the due share of the monastery lands. As a protest against this unseemly discord a sect was formed, whose members

B. E. 674.

B. E. 684.

---

[1] *Hist. Bur.*, p. 58.

[2] Thihathu (*Hist. Bur.*, pp. 59, 282). Bastian, *Gesch. Ind. Chin.*, p. 53.

[3] Panyā, a few miles to the north of Myinzaing. (*Hist. Bur.*, p. 59.)

[4] Son of the deposed Kyautswâ. (*Hist. Bur.*, pp. 60, 282.) Crawfurd's *Journal*, Appendix viii.

withdrew from the more social life of the vihāras and lived in the forests.

704 In 1342 UJĀNA abdicated in favour of his half-brother Kyocvā[1] (p. 85). Here a group of short tales enlivens the chronicle. The author seems almost to enjoy writing of a wrestling match or describing the king's swiftest horse, but the religious aim of these anecdotes is not quite clear. Kyocvā does nōt appear to have been a notable benefactor of religion. In his young days he had not a thought beyond hunting, till he was advised by Sakra, in a dream, to observe Uposatha, as a means of arriving at power and kingship. Later, when on the throne, he was the patron of Samaṇakuttakas and even had them in his service. But he was an auspicious prince; he captured the five white elephants promised by Sakra, and his extraordinary luck is (consistently with the general theory of re-birth), counted to him for merit.

713 The reign of his son KITTISĪHASURA[2] (1351 A.D.) or CATUSETIBHINDA is marked by the writing of some well-known works. Among others is mentioned the *Saddasāratthajālinī*, and a picturesque story is told of the author, Nāgita, or Khaṇṭakakhipa—so nicknamed from the oddly inauspicious opening of his religious life, when he was so unwilling to be taken to study with a bhikkhu that his father, by way of rebuke, threw the obstinate boy into a thorny bush.

The second Shân capital, Jeyyapura,[3] and its founder
685 SAṂ-KHA-YĀ-CO-YON[4] (1323 A.D.) are mentioned only with the remark that no books were written in the city. No

---

[1] KYOASWA or NGĀ-SÎ-SHENG (1342 A.D.). *Hist. Bur.*, pp. 60, 282.

[2] Kyoaswâ IV. *Hist. Bur.*, pp. 60, 282. Crawfurd's *Journal*, Appendix viii.

[3] Sagain, on the right bank of the Irawaddy.

[4] ATHENGKAYA (1322), a son of Thihathu, who died in that year. (*Hist. Bur.*, pp. 60, 283.)

record of the last forty years of the Shân dynasty appears in the Sâsanavaṃsa. A few sentences carry the history over the destruction of Vijayapura and Jeyyapura, in 1364, B. E. 726. to the opening of a new epoch with the foundation of Ratanapura [1] by SATIVA-RĀJĀ in the same year (p. 87).

The first episode set down in the religious record of the new capital is the "establishment" of religion by two theras from Ceylon, Sirisaddhammâlaṃkāra and Sīhaḷa-mahâsâmi, who landed at Kusima in 1429, bringing relics B. E. 791. from their country (p. 90).

Byaññа,[2] King of Pegu, refused to allow them to settle in his dominions, and they proceeded to SIRIKHETTA, where the King of Burma [3] gave them a splendid reception. On the arrival of the relics an earthquake took place, which made a deep impression on the people. The Ceylon theras settled in Mramma, and the spread of religion in the country is ascribed to them. Still, the earlier kings of Ratanapura had not neglected works of piety. MA-ṄA-KRI-COK [4] (1368 A.D.) rebuilt the celebrated B. E. 730. Ca-nah-khuṃ Cetiya, and bestowed on his tutor, Khema-

---

[1] Ava, at the confluence of the Irawaddy and Myit-nge, founded by THADOMINBYA in 1364. This prince, who was supposed to be of the ancient royal race of Burma, resolutely attacked the Shân power and made himself king. (*Hist. Bur.*, pp. 63, 64; *Ind. Ant.*, vol. xxii. p. 8.) He built pagodas in his new capital, but "he is denounced (says Phayre) in Burmese history as a man of cruel disposition who altogether disregarded religion." He reigned less than four years.

[2] BINYÂ-RÂN-KÎT (*Hist. Bur.*, pp. 83, 290).

[3] MENG-NÂN-SI (1426 A.D.), a Shân, who claimed descent from PAÑCA-SETIBHINDA (*Hist. Bur.*, p. 82).

[4] MENG-KYI-SWÂ-SOA-KAI, elected successor to THADOMINBYA in 1368. He left so great a reputation as a warrior that he is counted among the five kings of Burma whose conquests brought the most glory and territory to his country (Yule, *Mission to the Court of*

cara, whom he made head of the Order, the royal dignity of the white umbrella.

It is at this period—in the time of ADHIKARĀJĀ [1] (1400 A.D.)—that a *Saṃgharājā* is first mentioned in this chapter. Adhikarājā's tutor, on whom he bestowed the title, is expressly excluded by our author from the succession of theras; but the same king was fortunate in calling bhikkhus to his aid in temporal affairs. When RĀJĀDHIRĀJĀ,[2] King of Rāmañña, invaded his country and threatened his capital with a siege, it was a bhikkhu of his council who confidently undertook to parley with
l. 766. the foe, and exhorted Rājādhirājā to such purpose that he returned peaceably to his own country.

l. 788. In the following reign (that of MRIḤ-ÑA-ṄĀH, 1426 A.D.),[3] the era was changed and a new reckoning established (according to the old Burmese custom) to avert an evil omen. In the Sāsanavaṃsa the king is said to have been counselled by two learned theras to make the change; it is an interesting and (in our text) an unusual mention of theras acting as astrologers (their advice to the king is given on the strength of the *Vedasattha*). There is no hint that these two were wanting in sacred knowledge, though, in another passage, a distinction is severely made between the higher learning and secular science.

Among the theras who lived and wrote at Ratanapura in the fifteenth century, the most celebrated was Ariyavaṃsa (author of *Maṇisāramañjusā*, *Maṇidīpa*, *Gandhābharaṇa* and *Jātakavisodhana*). He is another example of a

---

Ava, p. 269; Bastian, *Gesch. Ind. Chin.*, p. 55; Phayre, *Hist. Bur.*, pp. 64, 284).

[1] MENG-KHAUNG, son of Meng-Kyi-swa-soa-kai (*Hist. Bur.*, pp. 70, 284).

[2] RĀJĀDIRIT came to the throne of Pegu 1385 (*Hist. Bur.*, pp. 68, 290). The Rājavaṃsa tells the same story.

[3] In Father San Germano's abridgement of the Rājavaṃsa (*Burmese Empire*, chapter viii.), SADDAMMARĀJĀ (1426 A.D.) changed the era because of an evil omen.

bhikkhu with that strong influence over the king, that the monks have known so well how to exercise and their chroniclers to describe. Ariyavaṃsa, the scholarly and magnaminous teacher, stands out, a dignified figure, in some anecdotes, that occur here, together with an interesting list of the works produced by different writers in this fruitful period. Among the literary theras two poets are mentioned, who are not counted by the authors of the *porāṇapotthakā* in the Succession of theras.[1]

A celebrated teacher in the reign of SIRITRIBHAVANĀDITYANARAPATIVARE[2] (1501 A.D.) was the Saddhammakitti, of whom we have already heard. His name is bound up with memories of the bitter persecution of the monks that followed the invasion of Burma by the Shâns early in the sixteenth century. B. E. 863.

Saddhammakitti withdrew for safety to Ketumatī with his pupils, one of whom, Tisāsanadhaja, was afterwards brought to Haṃsāvati[3] by King ANEKASETIBHINDA,[4] who was reigning over Pegu and Burma in 1551 A.D. Anekasetibhinda's predecessor, TA-BENG-SHWÈ-HTÎ[5] (1540 A.D.), B. E. 912.

---

[1] For further remarks on the writing and reciting of poetry by Samaṇas, Paññasāmi refers to his own book, *Uposathavinicchaya*, where he treats of the *sikkhāpada* relating to singing and dancing.

[2] SHWE-NAN-SHENG NARAPATI (1501 A.D.) [an error in my transcript, observed too late, places this king three years earlier]. In his reign Salun, the Shân chief of Monyin, "after years of desultory warfare," took Ava by storm, and the king was killed escaping from the city (*Hist. Bur.*, pp. 89, 285).

[3] Pegu city.

[4] BURENG NAUNG (called "Branginoco" by the Portuguese), 1551, King of United Pegu and Burma (*Hist. Bur.*, pp. 161, 290).

[5] Prince of Taungu, at the time of the Shân rule in Burma. He is reckoned as a descendant of the ancient royal race. He reigned ten years as "emperor" at Pegu (*Hist. Bur.*, pp. 93, 291).

is not mentioned, although he appears in the histories as a patriot and even "the recognised champion of the Burmese people." The Shân rule in Burma was broken in his successful campaigns, but his religious foundations were in Pegu, and would therefore be no concern of the Burmese saṃgha.

Very little is said of ANEKASETIBHINDA. It was in Rāmañña that he built cetiyas and vihāras, and the Europeans of his time who wrote of the dazzling splendour of his capital and court and the width of his dominion, speak of him as the "King of Pegu." From the faint trace left by this imposing personality in the Sāsanavaṃsa, we may suppose that religion did not suffer by the disturbed state of the country. Bureng Naung's activity was felt throughout the whole of Burma in his conquests and administration, and it is recorded of him that he even forced Buddhism on the Shâns and Muslim in the north of his kingdom.

Of Bureng Naung's son, Ñ̃O-NA-RA-MAḤ, or SĪHASŪRA-
. 961. DHAMMARĀJĀ[1] (1599 A.D.), we only hear that he restored Ava and was building cetiyas and vihāras when he met his death on his return from a victorious expedition to Theinni (or Sinni).[2]

Under his eldest son[3] the Order seems to have flourished

---

[1] NYAUNG-RÂM-MENG (1599 A.D.). *Hist. Bur.*, p. 286. He was a younger son of Anekasetibhinda, and tributary king of Ava.

[2] In the North Shân States, a little to the west of the Upper Salwen river (see *Hist. Bur.*, pp. 127, 128).

[3] MAHĀDHAMMARĀJĀ (1605 A.D.). *Hist. Bur.*, pp. 128, 129, 286. A notable feat of the king is passed over by our history. He successfully attacked Philip de Brito, the Portuguese Governor in Pegu, and avenged the wrongs done to the Order by "the sacrilegious wretch who destroyed Pagodas." This event, however, would touch the Saṃgha of Burma only indirectly, if at all, and its

both materially and intellectually, for a great number of works were written in the vihāras built by the king's bounty.

A few titles of poems and commentaries are given, and mention is made of two bhikkhus from Rāmañña, who were favoured by the king for their ability in temporal affairs (*lokadhammachekatāya*). As their science lay chiefly in the *Vedasatthas*, the ancient chroniclers do not reckon them in the Succession of theras; but the reputation they left, notwithstanding, is one of the signs of an undoubted revival of scholarship at this time, which showed itself, during the following reign, in a keen rivalry between the monks of Pegu and those of Burma.

King UKKAṂSIKA,[1] a famous patron of religion, had established his capital at Haṃsāvatī,[2] but had a jealous regard for the reputation of the Mramma scholars. Hearing that they were underrated in Rāmañña, he sent for learned theras from his own country, and caused a disputation to be held, in which, according to our author, the theras of Burma shone by such profound knowledge that even those of Rāmañña were forced to testify to the scholarship of the new-comers.

Ukkaṃsika returned to his Burmese subjects in Ratanapura in 1634.[3] In 1647 occurred an attempt upon his B. E. 1009.
life and throne, the story of which, as told in the Sāsanavaṃsa, is different from the Rājavaṃsa version of the same event, and shows the bhikkhus in a rather unusual character; in fact, as good fighters in case of need.

---

affairs are throughout kept rigidly apart from those of the Saṃgha of Pegu.

[1] THADODHAMMARĀJĀ (1629 A.D.), brother of Mahādhammarājā. The date given in the Sāsanavaṃsa is 1634, in which year Ukkaṃsika left Haṃsāvatī and established his capital at Ratanapura. (*Hist. Bur.*, pp. 134, 286.)

[2] *Hist., Bur.*, p. 134. [3] *Ibid.*, p. 135.

Paññasāmi's account of the affair is, briefly, as follows. In the year 1647, the king's younger brother[1] died. Then the king's son, the Prince of Uccanagara placed himself at the head of a conspiracy to dethrone his father, and forced his way into the palace. The king fled from the city, in disguise, bearing away some of the royal jewels, and accompanied by two of his ministers. They reached the river,[2] revealed the king's identity to a sāmaṇera, who was about to cross over, and induced him to give them a place in his boat. The sāmaṇera took them to his vihāra, where the royal fugitive threw himself on the protection of the superior. He was not only loyally received, and kept in hiding, but all the bhikkhus of the neighbourhood were called together and organised for a stout defence by one of the theras, who seems to have had some military experience when a layman. The vihāra was guarded by outposts of bhikkhus armed with staves; and the king's pursuers at last withdrew baffled and overawed. The attempted revolution failed, and the king, when restored to power, showed his gratitude to his defenders by gifts of vihāras (p. 109).

It is interesting to set against this story the summary of the Rājavaṃsa account given in Phayre's *History of Burma*.[3] "The conduct of Thadodhammarājā seems to have been irreproachable. Nevertheless, his life was endangered from a conspiracy, the leading features of which have been repeated in recent times. The Heir-Apparent having died, his son was discontented that he was not appointed to succeed to that office. He suddenly assembled a band of armed desperate men and forced his way into the palace. The king fled by the west gate, and

---

[1] The Heir-Apparent (according to Burmese custom) Mengre-Kyoaswâ.

[2] In this passage the Irawaddy is called the *Rajata-vāluka* (river of silver sand) instead of Erāvati, as elsewhere in the text.

[3] Pp. 135, 136.

took refuge in a monastery. *He then crossed the river and entered a stockade near Sagaing, which was guarded by soldiers.* The rebel prince having no influence in the country, a large body of men rallied round their sovereign. The prince came out of the city and was killed fighting. The king then returned to his palace, and all the men of rank who had been forced to join the rebels were, with their wives and children, burnt as traitors."

Among Ukkaṃsika's religious foundations are mentioned the Rājamaṇicūla Cetiya[1] and three vihāras, in one of which a certain learned thera wrote two grammatical works. The tutor to Ukkaṃsika's son and successor, SIRINANDADHAMMARĀJĀPAVARĀDHIPATI[2] (1648), at about this time, wrote a commentary on the celebrated grammatical treatise *Nyāsa*. B. E. 1010.

In the Sāsanavaṃsa we so rarely hear of popular movements and feelings that it is interesting to find a mention of evil omens occurring in 1650, and causing widespread anxiety and terror lest the guardian gods should be leaving the capital.[3] Though we have here a clear glimpse of Nât-worship, the omens had their bearing on the history of the Faith. It was at this time, says the historian, that the armies of the Emperor of China devastated Mramma,[4] and religion was dimmed as the moon by clouds. B. E. 1012.

---

[1] The "stupendous temple" known as the Kaung-mhu-doa, on the right bank of the river, five miles from Sagain (Crawfurd's *Journal*, vol. i. p. 346; Phayre, *Hist. Bur.*, p. 135.)

[2] Bengtalè (1648 A.D.) *Hist. Bur.*, p. 136.

[3] *Devatā* in text—the Pali equivalent for the Burmese *Nât*. Bishop Bigandet observes of the Nât-worship of Burma, that it is observed privately or publicly by all, from the king downwards, and, further, that it is formally inculcated by the monks. (*Life or Legend of Gaudama*, French edition, pp. 24, 77); see also Taw Sein Ko, *The Spiritual World of the Burmese.*)

[4] Burma was troubled from 1651 to 1661 by rumours of

Nevertheless in the reigns of MAHĀPAVARADHAMMARĀ-
S. 1013. JĀLOKĀDHIPATI[1] (1651) and his successor NARAVARA (1672)[2] we hear of the building of vihāras and the writing of books, and King SIRIPAVARAMAHĀDHAMMA-
S. 1034-5. RĀJĀ[3] (1673) evidently took a real interest in religion for he commanded that the *Paṭṭhānapakaraṇa*[4] should be preached (for the first time) in Mramma and also in Rāmañña. It was in his reign, we are told, that the custom was first introduced, in Mramma, of decorating the outside boards of MSS. with lacquer and gold in the fashion that obtains to-day. There is a note of bitterness in a general comment of the author here on the last five kings of the Ño-ṄRA-MĀH dynasty reigning in Ava.[5] In their indifference to religion they showed equal favour to worthy and unworthy bhikkhus, so that religion languished. Yet, he adds, the succession of theras continued unbroken—as indeed did the succession of heterodox teachers—the

---

wars with China and later raids of Chinese marauders, who even threatened Ava. (*Hist. Bur.*, pp. 136, 137; Bastian, *Gesch. Ind. Chin.*, p. 62.)

[1] An insurrection had followed on the king's supposed indifference to the sufferings of the people. It was headed by the Prince of Prome, who caused his brother to be drowned and was consecrated as Mahā Pawra Dhamma Rājā (1661). (*Hist. Bur.*, pp. 138, 286.)

[2] Son of Mahāpavaradhammarājā. He died within a year of his accession. (*Hist. Bur.*, p. 140.)

[3] Brother of Naravara. He was not a capable ruler and his reign was marked by a gradual decline of the monarchy in Burma. (*Hist. Bur.*, p. 140.)

[4] The seventh book of the Abhidhamma.

[5] That is, from NARAVARA (1672) to MAHĀDHAMMARĀ-JĀDHIPATI (1733). (*Hist. Bur.*, p. 286.) It was a disastrous period for Burma, with raids from the North, rebellion from the South, and a breaking-up of the state itself, till Ava was at last burnt to the ground by the Talaings in 1752.

handing down of the so-called *ācariyapaveṇi*. The two opposing elements in the Order were soon to be matched in a long and noteworthy struggle.

With the reign of SIRIMAHĀSĪHASŪRASUDHAMMARĀJĀ[1] (1698 A.D.) begins a new chapter in the history of Burmese B. E. 1060
Buddhism—the PĀRUPANA-EKAṂSIKA controversy.

The rise and many phases of the dispute are set forth at length by the author of the Sāsanavaṃsa. His account must be followed here, without such omissions as would give a false idea of the proportion this characteristic part bears to the whole, though the story is as tedious as those of all such contentions, where the importance of the issues is comprehensible only to the parties in the dispute. Yet here and there a convincing touch shows us that certain principles were fought for as well as mere matters of monastic propriety, and the Sāsanavaṃsa account (by an ardent *Pārupana*), gives us, if in a strong party spirit, an instructive view of a question that kept the Saṃgha in a state of ever-renewed strife for more than a century.

A thera named Guṇābhilaṃkāra had gathered round him a following, who were distinguished by going about in the village with one shoulder uncovered by the upper garment (p. 118). From their distinguishing mark, the one bared shoulder, this party came to be called the *Ekaṃsika* sect. Meanwhile the followers of four other teachers—Buddhaṅkura, Citta, Suṇanta, and Kalyāṇa—strictly observed the wearing of the upper garment on both shoulders, during the village rounds. These latter, from their habit of going clothed, were called the *Pārupana* sect.[2]

---

[1] Son of Siripavaramahādhammarājā. (*Hist. Bur.*, p. 286.)

[2] Prof. Rh. Davids has been kind enough to give me some interesting details of two sects in Ceylon at the present day (the *Buramāgama* and *Siyamāgama*) which correspond to the *Pārupana* and *Ekaṃsika* sects. The

On this difference in daily practice the whole controversy turns.

The Ekaṃsikas asserted that their custom had been taught by the thera Saddhammacārī, who had visited Ceylon (a warrant of orthodoxy). Moreover they bribed a layman of loose morals, who had quitted the Order, to write a book supporting their views. At the same time a further irreligious tendency showed itself in the Saṃgha: a bhikkhu at the head of another group busied himself in drawing away the forest-dwelling monks from their retired life and attracting them to his own vihāra.

The king now intervened, for the first time, and issued a decree, commanding the two sects to keep to their own precincts, observing their own respective customs, and leaving each other in peace. But in the reign of his
1074 successor, SETIBHINDA[1] (1712 A.D.), the quarrel revived. Ukkaṃsamāla, the leader of the Pārupanas, was able to prove that the Pārupana practice was supported by the ancient writers, while the Ekaṃsikas rejected it on the strength of their own party traditions (*ācariyapaveṇi*). (p. 120.)

The king appointed a tribunal of four theras, before whom the two sects were to set forth their arguments. But the arbiters were monks without learning in the Sacred Texts and Commentaries, merely courtiers aiming to please the king. The question thus remained unsettled. The Ekaṃsikas could not conquer, by reason of the real weakness of their cause, and the Pārupanas wisely lay low, since the enemy was strong for the time being.

Buramāgama, or Burma sect, wear the upper garment habitually over both shoulders and only bare the left shoulder as a mark of courtesy, in intercourse with others. The Siyamāgama (Siam sect) adopt the slightly more ostentatious fashion of having one shoulder always uncovered.

[1] *H*SENG-PHYN-SHENG (in *Rājavaṃsa* list, 1714 A.D. *Hist. Bur.*, p. 286), another of the insignificant kings of the declining dynasty. (*Hist. Bur.*, p. 140.)

Now was indeed hardly the time for the king to occupy himself with ecclesiastical questions. From a few abrupt words of the historian we learn that we have arrived at the moment of disaster for the long declining power of Burma. In the year 1751 A.D. the King of Rāmañña[1] B.E. 1113 gained a victory over Mramma, Ratanapura was sacked, and the king carried away captive to Haṃsāvatī.[2] But it does not appear that the political changes made any great difference to the religious world. The rule of one Buddhist king instead of another could by no means be fraught with the same dangers and terrors to the Order as a Shân raid or a Chinese invasion. So, in these troublous times, the head of the Pārupanas (the King's tutor, Ñāṇavara) wrote several books. The strife of the sects was meanwhile kept up by the attacks of Pāsaṃsa, the head of the Ekaṃsikas (p. 122). The superior of one of the great royal vihāras had been appointed *Vinayadhara*. But the king's weakness for a favourite had blinded him to the monk's unfitness for the responsibility, and as the king himself was only equal to issuing a decree that every bhikkhu in his kingdom should observe what rules of life he pleased, the religious difficulty remained as far from a solution as ever.

Of all that passed in the eventful two years following the sack of Ava we have the merest glimpse. It is in connection with a revival of religion rather than of a people's freedom that we hear how "the king who founded Ratanasikha"[3] swept the Talaing armies out of the land, and conquered Rāmañña and ruled over it. The work of ALOṂPRĀ[4] the patriot, who, obscure and almost

---

[1] BINYA DALA (1746 A.D.). *Hist. Bur.*, p. 145; Bastian, *Gesch. Ind. Chin.*, p. 64. [2] *Hist. Bur.*, p. 147.

[3] Or Ratanasingha (Shwê bô, or Montshobo) about 60 miles to the north of Ava (*Ind. Ant.*, vol. xxii. p. 28; *Hist. Bur.*, p. 150).

[4] ALAUNGH-PRÂ (vernacular rendering of the Pali *Bodhisatta*. See *Hist. Bur.*, p. 149, *et seq.*; Yule, *Mission*

single-handed, drew together the fragments of the broken state, and in two years raised Burma to a united nation, is recorded as a religious work—"Religion revived, so that the people of Mramma said, 'Our king is a bodhisat.'"

The king insisted on the observance of Uposatha by all his court, furthered the study of the Sacred Texts and supported the Saṃgha, and now the Pārupana-Ekaṃsika controversy entered on a new stage. The principal members of the Pārupana sect set forth their views in a

---

to the Court of Ava, p. 184). An incident in Alaungh-prâ's conquest of Pegu is thus related by Sir A. Phayre: "By the end of October (1756) the whole of Alaungh-prâ's army . . . had closed round the devoted city (Pegu). The King of Pegu had no resource left but to appeal to the mercy and the religious sentiment of his enemy—an expedient of which several instances are mentioned in the histories of the wars of Burma. The deeply revered Rahâns, headed by their venerable superior, appeared in the camp of the invader, and in the name of religion besought him to put an end to the war, and to live as elder and younger brother with the King of Pegu. In other words the kingdom was to be held as tributary to the King of Burma. The chief Rahân, in his address, with sincere or artful allusion to the conqueror as a destined Buddha, referred to the satisfaction he would feel in after ages when that high and holy state had been attained in his last birth, and when he could look back with pure delight on a noble act of generosity and mercy which would give relief to millions of human beings" (*Hist. Bur.*, p. 163). The venerable envoy was received with the respect that the kings seem always to have shown to the Order; but a further defence brought down on the Talaings the sack of the city and a slaughter, in which, according to the chronicles of Pegu, even the monks were not spared.

letter to the king. Thereupon the Ekaṃsikas (of whom Atula,[1] the king's tutor, was the leader), wrote to the king, asserting that the whole question had been settled in the time of his predecessors, and could not be raised again.

The king in reply declared that he was, just then, too much busied with state affairs to attend to religious matters, and shortly afterwards issued a decree that all bhikkhus were to conform to the practice of the royal *âcariya*. The order was generally obeyed, but two Pârupana theras of Sahassorodhagâma held staunchly to their principles, and continued to teach their following as before. Atula sent for these two to come to the capital, and tried to destroy their credit with the people, but his unjust dealing brought down on him a supernatural warning—a storm, in which thunderbolts fell on his own vihâra and the king's palace (p. 125).

A touch of vivid interest brightens here the monotonous story of the long, futile dispute. The them Munindaghosa observed and taught the Pārupana practice with unswerving steadfastness, in defiance of the royal prohibition and in despite of banishment. At last, with his life in his hand, he came to the capital and faced the formidable Aloṃprā. Neither begging the latter's mercy nor fearing his wrath he simply laid aside the monastic robe, and came as a layman, lest the grievous guilt of slaying a monk should be upon the king. "I have come hither, laying aside my vows, that this heavy sin might not be

---

[1] The "royal preceptor" (Atula Sayâdô) is mentioned in the Po: U: Daung Inscription of 1774. "He was the Thathanabaing or Buddhist Archbishop appointed by Alaungp'ayâ when the latter became king. Atula Sayâdô retained his office throughout the reign of five kings, and was removed by Bô-do-p'ayâ for his schismatic doctrines" (Taw Sein Ko, *Po: U: Daung Inscription of S'in-byu-yin. Ind. Ant.*, vol. xxii. p. 8).

thine. Now, if thou wilt slay me, slay!" he said. And Alompră dared not.

Alompră's last expedition to Siam[1] is mentioned. He died upon the homeward march (or rather the retreat),
1122 and was succeeded in 1760 A.D. by his eldest son
SIRIPAVARAMAHĀDHAMMARĀJĀ[2] (p. 127).

As the royal tutor (the learned grammarian and philosopher Ñāṇa) held the Pārupana views, the orthodox party now hoped to gain recognition. They laid a written memorial before the king, but their chief opponent, Atula, interposed as before, and prevented a fair hearing by a counter-declaration that the question had been already settled. Nothing noteworthy, it would seem, happened during the short reign of Siripavaramahādhammarājā. Under his successor, SIRIPAVARASUDHAMMA-
1125 MAHĀRĀJĀDHIPATI[3] (1763 A.D.) a certain heresy arose
and spread widely. What the heresy was we are not told, but only that the king forced the heretics to embrace the true religion.[4]

Of HSEN-BYN-SHENG we hear very little, though he was "an enlightened monarch," and "a staunch

---

[1] 1760 A.D. Phayre, *Hist. Bur.*, p. 168.

[2] NAUNG-DOA-GYI, *Hist. Bur.*, pp. 184, 287.

[3] HSENG-BYN-SHENG, the second son of Alaungh-prâ. (*Hist. Bur.*, pp. 186, 287.) [Erroneously dated at B.E. 1205 (1843 A.D.) in the Text.]

[4] A certain movement in the Burmese community is noticed by Spence Hardy in *Eastern Monachism* (1850) which may perhaps have been a revival of the "heresy" suppressed by HSENG-BYN-SHENG in the middle of the eighteenth century. "About fifty years ago a class of metaphysicians arose in Ava called Paramats, who respect only the Abhidhamma and reject the other books that the Buddhists consider as sacred, saying that they are only a compilation of fables. The founder of the sect, Kosan, with about fifty of his followers, was put to death by order of the king' (*op. cit.*, p. 331).

Buddhist."[1] The religious act commemorated in the Inscription at Prome,[2] namely, the crowning of the great pagoda at Rangoon—is not mentioned in the Sâsanavaṃsa. It is said of this king, however, that the Ekaṃsika heresy had no success under his rule.

When his son MAHÂDHAMMARÂJÂDHIRÂJÂ[3] (1776) mounted the throne, the Ekaṃsikas again approached the new king. SINO-GU-SÂ, who was under the influence of the orthodox thera Nandamâla, summoned both parties to hold an open disputation before him. The result was a crushing defeat for the Ekaṃsikas; whereupon the king commanded that all bhikkhus should instruct their sâmaṇeras in the orthodox practice. How far this decree succeeded we are not told; but the next king BONOAH PRÂ[4] (1781) was by no means content to let the religious question rest. He held that, as the disputation had been held in the palace, the one party had been intimidated or B.E. 1138 B.E. 1143

At least one connecting link may be pointed out here between this later school and the sect denounced by Paññasâmi—the Sâsanavaṃsa mentions that Guṇâbhilaṃkâra, the first leader of the Ekaṃsikas, "taught his pupils the *Abhidhamma*." Heresies of doctrine and practice were no doubt intermingled, all along, though we hear little of the former in our history. It is possible that Christianity, first introduced into Upper Burma in the 18th century, may be meant (see Bird's *Wanderings in Burma*, p. 88).

[1] Jas. Gray, *Dynasty of Alaung-Prâ*, p. 24. This author mentions that Hsen-byn-Sheng warmly encouraged the study of Sanskrit literature, and sent to Benares for Brahman scholars to come and live at his capital.

[2] The Po: U: Daung Inscription, *Ind. Ant.*, vol. xxii. p. 1.

[3] Sing-gu-sâ, who succeeded at the age of nineteen. For his short and futile reign and miserable death, see *Hist. Bur.*, pp. 207, 208, 209.

[4] Fifth son of Alomprâ. *Hist. Bur.*, pp. 208, 209, 287.

overawed, and had therefore suffered defeat. His plan was to send commissioners to the different monasteries that the theras might set forth their views to these latter, unhampered by any fears. The Captain of the Bodyguard was made head of the Commission of Inquiry. The Ekaṃsikas (perhaps upon a royal hint) [1] acknowledged to the king's commissioners that their practice was not supported by the scriptures, but only by tradition. The king, judging the question to be closed by this avowal, issued a decree commanding the observance of the rules laid down for sāmaṇeras by orthodox teachers.[2]

The founding of the new capital Amarapura in 1782 [3] is mentioned with the conventional prophecy supposed to have been uttered by the Buddha upon the site, in his lifetime. While Bodoah Prâ went about to expiate the bloodshed of the opening of his reign, and to build the "Immortal City" by the unpaid and unwilling labour of his subjects,[4] he was careful to assure himself a religious reputation in other ways. A list of vihāras (which, the author assures us, does not contain all, lest his book should be inordinately long) shows the splendid bounty of the king, the royal family, and the nobility of this time.[5]

---

[1] The king's own tutor was of the orthodox school; and from our knowledge of Bodoah Prâ's usual methods, we can hardly suppose that there was less intimidation in the "Inquiry" than in the open debate.

[2] *Parimaṇḍalasuppaticchanasikkhāpadāni* enjoin the entire covering of the person while walking abroad.

[3] *Hist. Bur.*, p. 211. Yule's *Mission*, p. 130 *et seq.*

[4] *Hist. Bur.*, pp. 210, 211. Father San Germano, *Burmese Empire* (ed. Jardine), p. 68.

[5] The light thrown on Bodoah Prâ's personality and acts by less partial writers, brings out a curious contrast between his religious zeal and his atrocious inhumanity and cruelty as a ruler. Father San Germano speaks with detestation of this king as a monster of wickedness, but notes that, in his time, it was a capital offence to drink

A step was made during this reign in the further organisation of the Saṃgha, at the head of which were four Saṃgharājās, under the Supreme Head of the Order. Four more were now added to the number. The king's Guru, Ñāṇābhivaṃsanadhaja, was made Supreme Head. He is said to have been very active in religious reforms, moving from vihāra to vihāra, teaching, practising ascetism, and writing books.

Two years after the founding of Amarapura, the Pārupana-Ekaṃsika dispute had been revived by the restless Atula, who sent a letter to the king maintaining that he had scriptural authority, in a text called *Cūlaganṭhipada*, for the practice of baring one shoulder and wearing a girdle round the body (p. 136). The king thereupon called together an assembly of Māhatheras to meet the champion of the Ekaṃsikas, and come finally at the truth.

This debate, in which Atula was put to utter shame and met with "threefold defeat," is described with great zest. The historian illustrates each "defeat" with a picturesque tale, to bring home to the reader the miserable confusion of the heretic and the triumph of his opponents. The triumph, this time, was final and complete for the orthodox party.

With the dramatic scene in the Council Hall ends the long-drawn-out story of the controversy. A royal command established the Pārupana practices for the whole of the kingdom, and, according to the author, they obtain everywhere to the present day (p. 142).[1]

---

wine, smoke opium, or kill any large animal. (*Burmese Empire*, ed. Jardine, p. 85.) Father San Germano's description is borne out by the royal history itself. (Phayre, *Hist. Bur.*, p. 230.)

[1] He adds that his account is only a summary, for if the whole controversy were related, with all the disputes and arguments on both sides, the Sāsanavaṃsa would be too tedious.

An important religious event at the opening of the present century was the rise of the so-called "AMARAPURA" school of Ceylon,[1] which, as Paññasāmi is careful to point out, owed its origin to the Burmese Saṃgharājā Ñāṇābhivaṃsa. He had bestowed ordination in the year
1162 1800 to a Siṅhalese deputation, headed by the thera Ambagahapati,[2] whose visit to Amarapura proved a strong feeling, existing in a part of the Ceylon community, that the unbroken succession of theras could only be secured by consecration in Mramma (p. 142).

Bodoah Prâ's later years are passed over in silence.[3] In

---

[1] Spence Hardy gives the chief tenets of the Amarapura School, whose aim was to restore the ancient purity of Buddhism. Among the principal points are, that this sect (1) allows ordination to all castes; (2) the members go about with both shoulders covered and eyebrows unshorn. (*Eastern Monachism*, pp. 328, 329.)

[2] The following account of this incident is given by Yule: "In the teeth of fundamental principles the privilege of admission to the Order was, in Ceylon, long confined to the highest caste. . . . In the end of the last century a bold candidate of low caste, with several like-minded companions, visited Amarapura in search of ordination. They were well received by the king and priests, were admitted to the Order, and, on their return to Ceylon in 1802, accompanied by several Burman priests, brought a missive from the Thathana Bain or Patriarch at Amarapura, to the corresponding dignitary at Kandy. Their community is known in Ceylon as the Amarapura Society, and they denounce the heterodox practices of the established body there." (*Mission to the Court of Ava*, p. 241.)

[3] It would be difficult for our historian to speak either of the king's pretensions to Buddhahood, which the Order refused to recognise, or the gigantic pagoda, begun by his command, which his deeply discontented subjects would

1819 his grandson SIRITRIBHAVANĀDITYAPAVARAMAṆḌITA[1] succeeded him. Three of this ruler's religious discussions with his ministers are recorded, two of which were of very practical interest, dealing with the ancient grants of land, &c.,[2] to the Saṃgha. The Ministers laid down the principle (based on the Vinaya and Aṭṭhakathā) that the Order could continue to claim all rights bestowed by donors in time past (such as a share of produce of the land granted, provision for the repairing of cetiyas, &c.) (p. 145.) B.E. 1181.

On another occasion Hpagyidoa asked in whose reign gifts of land, with cetiyas and vihāras, had first been bestowed on the Order. In this case, too, the minister consulted (who went back as far as the time of the Bhagavat Sujāta for a precedent) was able to answer to the king's satisfaction.

Hpagyidoa's later years, darkened by listless brooding over defeat[3] and narrowed territory, were not marked

---

not finish (see Father San Germano's account in *Burmese Empire*; Yule, *Mission to the Court of Ava*, p. 169; Phayre, *Hist. Bur.*, p. 219).

[1] Hpagyidoa (1819). *Hist. Bur.*, p. 287. "He commenced his reign well. He remitted some taxes for three years, and in a speech to his courtiers promised to rule justly and to follow the precepts of religion" (*Hist. Bur.*, p. 252).

[2] Bp. Bigandet says that according to inscriptions found at Pugân it is evident the monasteries and temples were endowed, in the palmy days of that city, with rice-fields, fruit-trees, cattle, &c.; but that no vestige of such acts of bestowal, dating within the last three or four centuries, has been found (see *Life or Legend of Gaudama*, p. 169).

[3] In the first Anglo-Burmese War (1824) he sank into inactivity and melancholy, and was at length dethroned by his brother, the Prince of Tharāwadi (*Hist. Bur.*, p. 260), who, himself, afterwards went mad.

1199. by any special benefits to the Saṃgha. In 1837 the reign of his younger brother SIRIPAVARĀDITYALOKĀDHIPATI began:[1] the only events recorded are the appointment, death, and funeral of the Saṃgharājā, the appointment of his successor (who wrote a commentary on the *Saddhammapajotikā*), and the arrival of another deputation from Ceylon (p. 147).

The accession of SIRIPAVARĀDITYAVIJAYĀNANTA[2]
1208. (1846 A.D.) seems to have fallen at the beginning of a period fruitful in religious literature. A great number of books were written; those mentioned by Paññasāmi are chiefly *Atthayojanas* in Burmese, on the Suttapiṭaka and commentaries. It is certain that the scholars of the Burmese community were deeply in earnest in their endeavour to make the ancient scriptures, the treasury of the purer, earlier Buddhism, accessible to the lesser learned, to whom *ṭikās* written in Pali would have taught nothing. The author of the Sāsanavaṃsa (whose name now appears, for the first time, as a pupil of the Saṃgharājā) praises with exaggerated, enthusiastic loyalty the king who next ascended the
1214. throne (p. 148), MENG-DUN-MENG[3] (1852), as the source of the religious revival of those days; but it is clear that the monks had already done their part of the work in writing and teaching before the righteous king was at the head of affairs. An immediate consequence, however, of the king's earnestness was that religion was zealously practised, in appearance at least, by the royal family, the court, and the people as a whole.

---

[1] Tharāwadi Meng (1837 A.D.), *Hist. Bur.*, p. 287; Yule's *Mission*, pp. 131, 226.

[2] PUGÂN-MENG (son of Tharāwadi) (1846 A.D.), of whom Sir *H*enry Yule says: "*H*e had all the worst parts of his father's character without the plea of insanity in excuse."

[3] Brother of PUGÂN-MENG, whom he deposed (*Hist. Bur.*, p. 287).

The historian rises literally into a song of praise [1] as he dwells on the virtues of the *dhammarājā* and the new enthusiasm for religion, in monks and laity alike. But already, a year after the festival of the founding of Ratanapuṇṇa [2]—Meng-dun-Meng's new capital — the general fervour seems to have cooled. Meng-dun-Meng learned with grief that signs of growing laxity were appearing in the Order. It was the old story—a departure from the primitive strictness of the precepts that the Master had laid down, to rule the bhikkhu's life. Some used gold and silver, others chewed betel-nut at unseasonable hours, drank forbidden beverages, and went into the villages, wearing shoes and carrying umbrellas. The king was anxious to impose a vow (*patiññā*) of abstinence from these indulgences, but, doubting if such a measure would be lawful, he consulted the Saṃgharājā. The Primate summoned a council of Mahātheras, and charged the king's minister to question them on their views (P. 155). Opinion was divided. The Saṃgharājā and some others held that the king would be justified (by his earnest desire for reform) in imposing the vow; but others were against it. Finally the Saṃgharājā called on his pupil Paññasāmi to set forth the views of the Head of the Order. The younger thera then delivered a discourse; taking as his

---

[1] *He* quotes here several verses from a poem of his own composition, the *Nagarājuppatti*. The poem shows that its author understands the courtly art of praising kings. It must be said that MENG-DUN-MENG won a tribute of high practice from many European writers, who judged him from a severer standpoint than his *ācariya*. It is generally agreed that he was an enlightened, just ruler, earnestly striving after the good of his people, and perhaps more true to the noble ideals of the religion he "supported" than any of his predecessors.

[2] Mandalay, founded 1857.

text passages of the *Vinaya*, *Pātimokkha*, *Parivāra*, and *Suttavibhaṅga*, and referring to Buddhaghosa's commentary, he argued that imposing a vow, in all sincerity, to restrain the monks from sin, would be a blameless act. He pointed out in how many religious acts the *patiññā* enters. Newly ordained bhikkhus, at the time of the *Upasampada* ordination, pronounce a solemn vow, on the exhortation of the upajjhāyas. In the same way novices (*sāmaṇerā*) at the moment of renouncing the world (*pabbajjā*) take a vow to observe the Precepts; bhikkhus, when acknowledging a fault committed, continually take a vow of amendment; novices, when entering upon their training under an *upajjhāya*, take a vow; and the vow the king wished to impose did not differ from these, solemnly sanctioned by scripture and by precedent.

The assembly was convinced, the king acted on its judgment, and the laxer members of the Order returned, under compulsion, to a stricter way of life (p. 158).

We now come to the last controversy, perhaps recorded because it points to the influence of the Burmese Saṃgha in Ceylon (p. 159). An ancient *Sīmā* in the island was the subject of dispute. One party in the Sinhalese Saṃgha maintained that consecration performed within this boundary was not valid, as the *Sīmā* was no longer fit in every respect for the ceremony.[1] Another party

---

[1] The fault of the *Sīmā* in question was *Saṃkāradosa*, *i.e.*, confusion (of boundaries), because a causeway had been built connecting it with others (*cf.* the discussion on the validity of *Sīmās* for ordination in the Kalyāṇi Inscriptions where the phrase occurs: "Apare tu therā: dvinnam baddhasīmānaṃ yeva rukkhasākhādisambandben' aññamaññasaṃkāro hoti . . . ." [Text of Kal. Ins. by Taw Sein Ko, *Ind. Ant.*, vol. xxii. p. 155; *Translation*, vol. xxii. pp. 15, 29, *et seq.*] The complete purification of the space for ceremonies is a vital point, hence the importance of well-defined boundaries.

held that the *Sīmā* fulfilled all requirements, and the matter was brought for judgment to the Saṃgharājā at Mandalay, by deputations (with a short interval of time) from both sides.

They were hospitably received, vihāras were built for them, and the Saṃgharājā gave judgment, after consulting various books. The members of both deputations received presents from the king, and those who had been proved in the wrong were safeguarded (against a break in the succession of theras) by reordination.

A few ecclesiastical details of slight interest, that need not be brought into this review, bring the record up to the year 1860, when the History of Religion in Aparanta closes.

CONCLUSION.

The *History of Religion in Mramma* is, as we have seen, nothing more than the history of the Buddhist Order in SUNĀPARANTA and TAMBADĪPA. The record takes us beyond these limits in two periods only, that is when Taungu, under a king of Burmese descent, represented the older state (Aparanta being at that time under Shân rule), and later, when the kings of Burma, as "Emperors of Pegu," held their Court at Haṃsāvatī. But the record of the two Irawaddy provinces cannot be called a "local" chronicle, for the history of the Burmese as a nation centres in a group of cities on the upper river—PUGÂN, SAGAIN, AVA, PANYÂ, AMARAPURA, MANDALAY—each, in its turn, the seat of kings. In the monasteries and cetiyas of the capital has been reflected, more or less faithfully, the welfare of the country. Of necessity they prospered or suffered, in some degree, according as Burma triumphed over neighbouring states or suffered invasion, raid, and plunder from China, the Shân tribes, and Pegu.

Such glimpses of the times as occur in the Sāsanavaṃsa, and the dates, which serve as a guide through a crowd of anecdotes and digressions, agree, on the whole, with the secular history of Burma; but there are some significant omissions. The invasion of the Mongol armies of KUBLAI KHAN and the taking of the capital in 1284 A.D. are passed over in absolute silence; and this is only one example among many that might be brought forward. Some kings are altogether ignored, and those whose "merit" assures them a place in the religious chronicle are often shadowy figures, or are painted in colours that give the lie to history. In the Sāsanavaṃsa we hear of the pious zeal of KYOCVĀ and the bounty of BODOAH PRĀ. Yet we cannot do more than guess at the real greatness of ALOṂPRĀ, and we hear nothing of the tyranny and crimes of his successors—the hideous cruelty of one, the downright insanity of another. Nowhere does a single hint occur of the appearance of the Portuguese in Burma, or the later advance of the English into the heart of the old kingdom. Yet we know, from passages in the Sāsanavaṃsa itself—not to speak of European testimony—that monks have been, for centuries, advisers of the sovereign, peacemakers and negotiators in affairs of state. Mere ignorance and pious seclusion from the world are no explanation of the omissions in the Sāsanavaṃsa. The historian knows the relations—often shameful and grim enough—of the kings to their kinsfolk, subjects, and neighbours, but it does not come within his plan to set them down.

It is in this very one-sidedness of the record that lies no small part of its interest. While isolating the religion of the rulers from their political and private lives, it brings before us a picture of the relations of State and Saṃgha in Burma for eight centuries, from the time of ANURUDDHA, with his constant adviser, *Arahanta*, to the time of MENG-DUN-MENG, with his council of Mahātheras.

Those relations may be briefly summed up as a mutual dependence. The Order, though enriched by the gifts of pious laymen, yet depends, in the last resort, upon the king. Under such despotic rule no man's property or labour is his own; the means of supporting the Saṃgha may be withdrawn from any subject who is under the royal displeasure. The peaceful, easy life dear to the Burmese bhikkhu, the necessary calm for study or the writing of books, the land or water to be set apart for ecclesiastical ceremonies (a fitting place for which is of the highest importance), all these are only secured by the king's favour and protection. If this be borne in mind, the general loyalty of the Saṃgha to the head of the State is easy to understand. On the other side, the king's despotism is held in check and his religious feelings (if they exist at all) sharpened by expediency, or their place (if they are non-existent) supplied by the strongest motives of self-interest. At the lowest, the royal gifts of vihāras and the building of cetiyas are either the price paid down for desired prosperity and victory, or the atonement for bloodshed and plunder; and the despot dares not risk the terrors, the degradation, that later births, in coming time, may hold in store for him, if he injures or neglects the Saṃgha.

It would be a totally false view, however, to see in this mutual dependence only mutual bargaining. It cannot be doubted that many of the kings have been swayed by a real reverence for the sublime ideal of the Religion, and a real awe before the silent, impalpable power facing their own. And—for the monks—the Sāsanavaṃsa bears witness again and again to the noble indifference of members of the Order to kingly favour or disfavour. More than one strong protest is recorded, even against the building of a cetiya, by forced labour, and gifts to the Order, wrung from the misery of the people, have been steadfastly refused.

As a general rule, the king seems to have had a great and recognised authority in ecclesiastical affairs. The record (within historical times) begins with ANURUDDHA'S vigorous reforms. In later centuries we find the sovereign commanding teachers hither and thither, at his pleasure, and even enforcing the study of this or that branch of sacred learning. Though the development of the hierarchy in Burma to its modern form [1] is not distinctly traced in the Sāsanavaṃsa the nature of the Saṃgharājā's office is very clear. *H*e is no elected *H*ead of the Order, but appointed by the king, whose favourite, and tutor he usually is, and on whose death or deposition

---

[1] Bishop Bigandet, *Life or Legend* (French edition), pp. 477–480.

he will, most often, be replaced by the *âcariya* of the successor. Finally, it appears, from the accounts of controversies such as the great PÂRUPANA-EKAṂSIKA dispute, that the sovereign's power to settle a religious question by royal decree is fully recognised by the Saṃgha; while, to keep the balance of mutual dependence, we see the king himself usually under his *âcariya's* influence, so far as to ensure his favouring the orthodox or unorthodox school, according to the views of the Saṃgharâjâ.

The controversies of which we read in the Sâsanavaṃsa have their interest from another point of view. They illustrate not only the influence of the king in the affairs of the Order, but the whole character of the Buddhism of Burma.

It was said by Bishop Bigandet, many years ago (and by many writers since his day), that the Buddhism of Burma has kept the primitive character lost in other countries (as Nepâl); and this is well borne out by the religious annals of Mramma. Here we find, at least, a consistent striving carried on, century after century, to uphold the precepts and to keep before the bhikkhus of later times the earliest ideal.

That controversies have raged only too often over the veriest trifles, is the first and irresistible impression that the reading of these records brings with it. But strictness in details is, in itself, no departure from the spirit of the ancient and pure Buddhism. The "Discipline" of the Order embodies countless rules on the smaller decencies of life, which are ascribed to the watchful wisdom of the Master himself. *Here*, of course, the individual point of view of the author has to be taken into account, besides his monastic standing. *Heresy*, for Paññasāmi, means, before all, a falling away from the ancient Discipline; the controversies *he* records as noteworthy turn, for the most part, not on philosophical subtleties but on daily life,—on the precepts of the VINAYA rather than on the questionings of the KATHĀVATTHU.

The individual bias is clear, too, in the interesting, if short, notices of the literary history of Burma, contained in the Sāsanavaṃsa. The author's great delight, as a scholar, is in grammar. *H*is anecdotes of theras celebrated in this branch of learning, or of keen-witted women disputing with monks on Pali accidence, sound a note of real enthusiasm. It is a pious enthusiasm too; according to the orthodox, scriptural warrant is everything, in the settlement of religious difficulties. From the word of the ancient texts, expanded in the AṬṬHAKATHĀ and further explained by *ṭīkas* and *atthayojanas* there is no appeal. So the actual "word" becomes the rock on which right-believing and right-living rest, and generation after generation of teachers devotes itself passionately to the study of the Pali grammar. The "science of words" is held to be vital to the cause of Truth, and the writing of grammatical treatises rises to the height of a religious duty.

The Sāsanavaṃsa can be fairly judged only by hearing in mind the express and declared purpose with which the book was written. The author's first aim is to trace the *Theraparamparā*,—the spiritual pedigree of orthodox Buddhist teachers from the Master's own disciples downwards. Like the tie of blood between father and son is the relationship between each teacher and the pupil who is his direct successor. The succession depends on (1) Personal relation with the teacher as his pupil (*sissa*) and companion (*saddhivihārika*); (2) valid ordination; (3) strict orthodoxy—another name for the doctrine professed by the Vibhajjyavādins, who already claimed, in Açoka's day, to uphold the true teaching of the Master against encroaching heresies; (4) holiness of life, or "modesty" (to translate literally the characteristic phrase of the Buddhists). The *alajjībhikkhu* is no more to be reckoned in the *Theraparamparā* than is the *adhammavādī*.

Already, in the opening chapter of the Sāsanavaṃsa, the first two centuries of Buddhism are no sooner passed in review than the author turns back to follow the succession of theras from Upâli, the Master's own *saddhivihârika* to Mahâ-Moggaliputtatissa, from whom down to the present time the line of orthodox teachers, each inheriting his master's authority, is held to have been uninterrupted. And throughout the book we see an underlying purpose, even in the anecdotes, haphazard and irrelevant as some of them at first appear to be. That purpose is to separate the orthodox from the unorthodox (or even doubtful) theras, and to prove their claim to descent, in unbroken line, from the great teachers of the past. But, in fulfilling this purpose for Buddhist readers, the History of Religion brings the Saṃgha before us as no priestly caste nor even a community bound by necessarily life-long vows, but a brotherhood in touch with every class in the nation, sharing its activities, its feelings, many of its weaknesses.

It is not too much to say that the highest interest of the Sâsanavaṃsa lies rather in its reflection of the spirit than its history of the career of Buddhism in Burma. We value what the writer unconsciously reveals, rather than his dates, which are sometimes doubtful, or events, which are often fantastically wide of the truth. Even the orthodox prejudices woven into the work, and certainly the national traditions and local details with which it is coloured lend it a worth of its own. Its very narrowness brings us, by a direct way, the closer to this strange and great religion, so typical in itself of the Indian genius, yet planted in the midst of non-Indian races and secure—with roots deep in a past of many centuries; secure, in spite of ineradicable folk-superstitions and even reconciled with them.

We see in the religious History of Mramma a striking departure from the Master's conception of the true *Samaṇa*, the monk-philosopher, with his intense spirituality, his rapt calm, his abandonment of joy and sorrow, his love for all beings, and his detachment from all. Yet we find, too, a certain abiding fidelity to the Discipline and an earnest teaching of the Law of Gotama. We see the Order growing and changing to a hierarchy, relaxing its strictness of renunciation, so that its higher members become councillors of State or dignitaries of a Church supported and enriched by royal bounty; but we must recognise, besides, in all its ranks, a social force, an upholder of humanity and justice against barbaric tyranny, a grave, strenuous influence in the midst of a careless people, teaching the love of learning and compelling the obeisance of kings. We see the land loyal to the Conqueror it has never wholly understood, and none the less loyal, though the old gods still people every tree and stream and watch over every village. The chronicler's intimate knowledge, with all its limitations, comes to the aid of the more critical historian; the Burmese monk, busied in his quiet *kyaung*, lends help that cannot be foregone, if the history written from the outside point of view is to be no less just in its judgments than true as a record of facts.

LIST OF PRINCIPAL AUTHORITIES CONSULTED.

Bastian (Adolf), *Geschichte der Indo-Chinesen.*

Bergaigne (Abel), *L'Ancien Royaume de Campâ.*

Bigandet, *Life or Legend of Gaudama.*

Bird (Geo.), *Wanderings in* Burma.

British *Burma Gazetteer.*

Burney, *J. R. A. S., Bengal, &c.*

Childers (R. C.), Pali *Dictionary.*

Crawfurd (John), *Journal of an* Embassy *to the* Court *of Ava.*

Forbes, British *Burma.*

Forchhammer (Emil), (*a*) *Reports* (*Archæological, &c.*) *to the* British *Government.*

(*b*) *Early* History *and* Geography *of* British Burma.

(*c*) *Jardine Prize Essay on Buddhist Law in* Burma, *&c.*

Fournereau (Lucien), *Le Siam Ancien.*

Garnier (Francis), *Voyage d'Exploration en* Indo-*Chine.*

Gray (James), *Nīti* Literature *of Burma, &c.*

Hardy (Spence), (*a*) *Manual of* Buddhism.

(*b*) Eastern *Monachism.*

Kern, *Manual of* Indian *Buddhism.*

Köppen, *Religion des* Buddha.

Lassen (Chr.), *Indische Alterthumskunde.*

Lévi (Sylvain), (*a*) *La Grèce et* L'Inde.

(*b*) *Notes sur les Indo-Scythes, &c.*

Minaev (Ivan), *Recherches sur le* Bouddhisme.

Müller (Ed.), Pali Proper Names (*J. P. T. S.*), *&c.*

Oldenberg (H.), (A) *Vinayapitakam.* (B) *Vinaya Texts, &c.*

Pavie, *Mémoires et Documents de la Mission Pavie.*

Phayre (Arthur), *History of Burma.*
Rhys Davids (T. W.), (*a*) *Buddhism.*
(*b*) *Schools of Buddhist Belief, &c.*
San Germano, *The Burmese Empire* (Jardine's edition).
Taw Sein Ko, *Indian Antiquary*, vols. xxii., xxiii., &c.
Turnour (Geo.), *Mahāvaṃsa.*
Waddell (L.), *Buddhism of Thibet.*
Yule (Henry), *Mission to the Court of Ava.*
De Zoysa (Louis), *Report on the Inspection of Temple Libraries in Ceylon.*

UNWIN BROTHERS, PRINTERS, WOKING AND LONDON.